Praise for *An Unlikely Guru*

I love this book! Through sharing his nine awakenings, Chick explores how his deepest life questions became an essential part of his everyday living. He shows that no matter how busy we are and how many responsibilities we have, there is room for us to wonder and be curious about the very nature of our being. There is room to nurture what is most important to us.

It is exciting how the rich resources of the world's diverse meditative traditions have become so available to us, giving a wide perspective on how to attend to our deepest questions. They suggest that we don't need to turn to ideas and beliefs to find our way. They invite us to pause and look directly into our very nature. To become immersed in this timeless moment of being and discover who we really are--what we have always been.

Chick inspires us with his very human journey of discovery and awakening to his own nature, weaving in the wisdom of many meditative traditions and contemporary meditative explorers. He invites us to plunge in and nurture our own deepest questions--and to discover our own awakenings.

—Richard Witteman
Meditation teacher, Springwater Center for Meditative Inquiry

Once upon a time not too long ago, Chick and I scaled the Peruvian Salcantay Peak together—at 15,090 feet, far above Machu Picchu—along with a pretty tough crew of hikers. Along the way, a shaman invited us to plunge into an icy stream accompanied by the shaman's music. Chick alone accepted the invitation.

This is Chick Atkins, a man who lives with intensity and intention, who loves hard, commits fully, always seeks his truth—and most impressively of all, endows those around him with confidence in their paths as well.

Always his own man, he is also Everyman.

You may not scale the Andes, but in life, you scale your own treacherous peaks and face daunting unknowns. In *An Unlikely Guru*, Chick meets the unknowns of everyday life, both great and small, with trailblazing passion, awakening curiosity, and respect for the dignity of all human experience.

An Unlikely Guru is the story of Chick Atkins, who integrates the spiritual path and its insights into his everyday life better than anyone I know. In this highly entertaining book, he recounts his journey in a relatable way and shows how enlightenment is possible for any of us.

—Steve Denholtz
CEO, Denholtz Properties

an unlikely
guru

Chick Atkins

an unlikely
guru

How a Neurotic Jewish Real Estate Developer from New Jersey Found Enlightenment

(And How You Can, Too)

Advantage | Books

Published by Advantage Books, Charleston, South Carolina.
An imprint of Advantage Media.

ADVANTAGE is a registered trademark, and the Advantage colophon is a trademark of Advantage Media Group, Inc.

Printed in the United States of America.

10 9 8 7 6 5 4 3 2 1

ISBN: 978-1-64225-569-0 (Paperback)
ISBN: 978-1-64225-472-3 (Hardcover)
ISBN: 978-1-64225-471-6 (eBook)

Library of Congress Control Number: 2023908139

Cover design by Matthew Morse.

Advantage Books is an imprint of Advantage Media Group. Advantage Media helps busy entrepreneurs, CEOs, and leaders write and publish a book to grow their business and become the authority in their field. Advantage authors comprise an exclusive community of industry professionals, idea-makers, and thought leaders. For more information go to **advantagemedia.com**.

TO ELLEN:

best decision I ever made.

TO DAN, CORY, AND JAMIE:

you make the journey all worthwhile.

Contents

Acknowledgments

LET ME START BY THANKING all those who influenced, helped, and guided me along the path to spiritual insight. As you will realize from reading this book, I'm skeptical of the word "spiritual." It's used so widely and differently these days that it doesn't have much meaning left. Nonetheless, there are many great spiritual teachers out there today and sprinkled through human history.

Reading J. Krishnamurti opened my eyes to a whole new possibility of how to experience the world. Seeing him at Carnegie Hall before he died was an unforgettable experience. Zen Master Seung Sahn and his student Zen Master Richard Shrobe introduced me to the mystery and beauty of Zen meditation and philosophy, although I only played at being a student of Zen. It has never been my nature to just "follow the one path," as Jack Kornfield suggested; I prefer to see the wisdom and truth pointed to in all paths.

So it was that I came to Toni Packer and the wise and wonderful teachers at the Springwater Center for Meditative Inquiry. It felt like a spiritual home for my personality—nondogmatic, questioning what's going on without settling on easily digestible answers. Special thanks to the teachers there carrying on Toni's legacy who have become my friends over the years, particularly Wayne Coger, Sandra Gonzalez, and Richard Witteman.

Many thanks to others who helped me understand the process of awakening and its aftermath: Adyashanti, who provided the spark when it was needed, and Scott Kiloby, Francis Lucille, Rupert Spira, Loch Kelly, to name a few.

My deep gratitude to Dr. Robert Evans, who provided profound therapeutic guidance when I didn't even realize how much I needed it.

Thanks to the many incredible friends I made in Recovery, too many to mention but beautiful and wise are all of you, and your guidance to the path of self-understanding has been invaluable. Lew Abrams, so grateful for your friendship and advice when it was needed, and Tom P., I am inspired by your level of spiritual and emotional insight. To my Friday-morning meditation group friends, the fact that you keep showing up each week so we can bring the true spirit of community to each other truly enriches my life.

Thanks to all the folks at Advantage / Forbes Media who helped this dream of a book become reality. Patti Boysen for those first conversations that slowly chipped away my initial skepticism. When I told you I had no interest in writing a book about business success but that I would consider a book about life, particularly about combining a "traditional" life of family and business with a life of spiritual searching, your early encouragement kept me engaged. To Caroline Moore, my editor, who from the moment she got involved with the book has provided enthusiastic support and great suggestions.

Joe Kita, my cowriter, what can I say? Simply no way this book gets written without you—from writing a fantastic initial book plan that made me sit up and think *Wow, this could really happen!* to my having the good sense to ask if you would partner with me. Your professionalism, skill, and intelligence are all over this book, not to mention your unwavering calmness in the face of my passionate ramblings while waving my arms to make a point. Working with you has been an absolute pleasure.

Thanks to my many great friends, especially Steve Denholtz for your lifelong friendship; and Stew, your spiritual search enlightened my own many times along the way. Dave Eames, rest in peace, my friend, and please be there when I die to inform me what's really going on, as you did in life.

Special thanks to Barry Mandelbaum, Michael Lewis, Tony Pentz, Bruce Kleinman, and the late Paul Rosenberg, all professionals par excellence: your friendship and business guidance helped us get through difficult times and flourish during the good ones.

Thank you to my loving and wonderful parents, Steve and Alice, who aren't here to read this book but I hope are together again in eternity somewhere. To my brothers; Jack, who left us too soon; Dick, our loving relationship has been a constant support; and Bob, our brotherly love, friendship, and incredible partnership all these years has been a priceless gift. My wonderful sisters-in-law, Melanie, Joanna, and Lisa, and all my nieces and nephews, each of you a unique and beautiful soul whom I love. All of Ellen's family, Mike, Christie, all the amazing aunts, uncles, and cousins who immediately took me in as one of their own.

Dan, Cory, and Jamie, it is hard to put into words the love and joy you inspire in me. It is happiness itself to be able to love in the way that I love you. You are each great men in your unique way: self-aware, spiritually wise, caring, and compassionate, with a great sense of humor and what is truly meaningful in life. I feel I did something good for the world by playing a part in bringing each of you into it.

Last, but always first in my heart, Ellen. Best decision I ever made. I am one of the lucky ones who really found a soulmate for this journey of life. Everyone who knows you is touched by your infectious joy and passion for helping others find their own. Thank you for marrying me. The *real* Suburban Monk!

P.S. To Dexter, Murphy, and Sawyer. If you want unconditional love, look to your dogs. As Will Rogers said, *"If there are no dogs in heaven, then when I die I want to go where they went."*

If the only prayer you ever say is "thank you," that would be enough.

—MEISTER ECKHART, CHRISTIAN MYSTIC

■ ■ ■

One great question underlies our experience, whether we think about it consciously or not: What is the purpose of life?

… I believe that the purpose of life is to be happy. From the moment of birth, every human being wants happiness and does not want suffering. Neither social conditioning nor education nor ideology affect this.

… From my own limited experience I have found that the greatest degree of inner tranquility comes from the development of love and compassion.

—TENZIN GYATSO, THE FOURTEENTH DALAI LAMA

Foreword

I'D LIKE TO INTRODUCE you to Charles Atkins. His nickname is Chick, and he's a sixty-six-year-old Jewish real estate developer from New Jersey. He's passionate and a bit neurotic, and he reminds me of comedian and television producer Larry David—in both physical appearance and personality. Chick is the antithesis of the traditional spiritual guru. He spends his days in business clothes rather than a robe and sandals. His hair is thinning, not long and flowing. His last name has just two syllables and is easily pronounceable. He has never lived in a small stone hut in the Himalayas; nor does he collect crystals or read auras. All his insights have required eyeglasses. And he refers to himself as a "Jew Bu," which is short for Jewish Buddhist and meant to be self-deprecating.

In many respects, Chick is just like you and me. He's been married to Ellen for nearly forty years, and together they've raised three sons. Over the years, Chick has experienced all the normal joys, sorrows, stresses, frustrations, and blessings that life usually bestows. He admits to being flawed and indulging in drugs and alcohol, before spending eighteen years in recovery. In other words, he is human—just another guy behind the wheel you might glimpse in traffic, or someone at the gym or supermarket you nod hello to in passing. Nondescript.

But Chick is different in one significant way.

Chick is "awake."

I know, I know. I was skeptical when I first met him too. He wanted to write a book about his spiritual journey—part memoir for family and friends, part guidebook for anyone who is searching. His publisher had hired me to interview him and create a book plan. Besides being an author and editor myself, I'm also a yoga teacher and have long been interested in spirituality and meditation. I'd read the Tao Te Ching, *A Course in Miracles*, *Man's Search for Meaning*, and many other classics (although I can't say I completely understand them). I'd been to India, taken yoga classes all over the world, and attended workshops/retreats at Kripalu and Canyon Ranch, where I was fed new age wisdom in gluten-free amaranth wraps.

So, on our initial Zoom call, when Chick started talking about the different "awakenings" he'd experienced on his lifelong journey to "enlightenment," I tried to be polite and professional and resist any eye-rolling. I mean, he was so different from my idea of a classic guru that I, too, was dubious. In fact, if I remember correctly, he excused himself from the interview to quiet his barking dog and go to the bathroom. (Somehow, I thought gurus were above that!)

But eventually, as I listened to Chick, I had a bit of an awakening myself. The chief reason my interest in spirituality has remained just an interest and never evolved into anything more is because much of what's written and preached isn't practical for me. I respect the message, but My Truth is I'm simply too busy. It's one thing to bliss out during an occasional weekend yoga retreat, but if I did that routinely in the real world, I'd quickly be overwhelmed by all of life's responsibilities. Yet here was an ordinary guy still very much in the rat race who claimed to be enlightened (on some level) and integrating that sensibility into everyday life. Maybe he did have something to say after all. Maybe he was a different kind of sage for a new age.

Before I go any further, I should establish what it means to be awake. It is not the same as being "woke." It has nothing to do with politics or race. No, the "awakening" that Chick is referring to has more in common with its traditional definition—an arising from sleep, an opening of the eyes, a letting in of light.

To be awake is to be aware and to know that you are aware. It involves seeing and experiencing yourself and the world as they truly are, which is far different from what most of us think they are. It is a new level of comprehension and understanding, a transcendence that leads to greater peace and happiness.

Rarely does awakening come in one big blast. It's not like Wile E. Coyote pushing an Acme detonator on the unsuspecting Road Runner. Rather, it typically arrives in short flashes of insight that can be years or even decades apart—small aha moments where we glimpse how things really work and what they mean. Where these insights come from or why they happen when they do is a mystery. If they have anything in common, it's that they never call beforehand. They just show up bearing a deep truth. The experience is impactful, and most people never forget it. But because we live in such a hectic world, most of us never apply it. It gets pushed to the back of our cluttered-garage minds because to do anything more would require too much effort and time.

This is Chick's point of differentiation.

Despite years of meditation, attending numerous retreats with Eastern and Western masters, and reading countless books on enlightenment, Chick hasn't given in to the temptation (as many do) of using spirituality to *escape* ordinary life. Instead, he's used it to *embrace* ordinary life. His spirituality is grounded in reality.

Chick enjoys quoting from different sources to illustrate his points and to show that the Truths he's awakened to are not his own but universal. They are timeless, not new and improved. The book that inspired him to start meditating, *Everyday Zen* by Charlotte Joko Beck, begins in this wonderfully contrarian way:

> *Successful living means functioning well in love and work, declared Sigmund Freud. Yet most Zen teaching derives from a monastic tradition that is far removed from the ordinary world of romantic and sexual love, family and home life, ordinary jobs and careers. Few Western students of Zen live apart in traditionally structured monastic communities. Most are preoccupied with the same tasks as everyone else: creating or dissolving a relationship, changing diapers, negotiating a mortgage, seeking a job promotion. But the Zen centers that serve such students often retain an aura of esoteric specialness and separateness. Black robes, shaved heads, and traditional monastic rituals may reinforce the impression of Zen as an exotic alternative to ordinary life, rather than ordinary life itself lived more fully.... If Zen is to become integrated into Western culture, it requires a Western idiom: "Chop wood, carry water" must somehow become, "Make love, drive freeway."*

What Joko Beck is advocating—making spirituality practical— isn't easy to pull off. It means being conscious in an unconscious world.

And therein lies the challenge and the promise of this book. As Chick will fully explain, you don't need to become a different person, or even a better person, to wake up. You just need to realize that your life situation does not define you. On paper, Chick is a sixty-six-year-old Jewish real estate developer from New Jersey. But in reality he is much more than any description, no matter how detailed, can convey. You can probably sense this in yourself too. I know I do. We are all pieces of something grand—our life is *all* life—and awakening is simply becoming more cognizant of that. In fact, it's our natural state. We are already awake. We've just dulled our alertness with too much thinking, worrying, and planning. But the good news, and Chick's inspirational message, is that the solution does not lie in trying. Rather, it resides in surrendering—to just being who and what we naturally are.

There will be times while reading this book that you will knit your brow and say, "Huh?" That may have just happened now. But that's also natural. It's okay to be confused. You may not "get it" now, but you will.

This book is part memoir and part manual. In other words, in the personal is also the prescription. Instead of chapters, it's divided into nine Awakenings. As you proceed chronologically through Chick's life, you'll learn how each of his occurred and shed more light on who he is. Some of these Awakenings may be familiar; you may have already experienced a few. But everyone's journey is unique. Yours may be quite different.

Will this book lead you to enlightenment? That is not the point. You can't pursue or achieve something you already are. You can recognize or realize it, however, and *that* is the point. Enlightenment is simply living moment to moment, amid all the usual nonsense, with as much awareness and appreciation as possible. This is why Jack Kornfield entitled one of his best-selling books *After the Ecstasy, the Laundry.*

Chick decided to write this book not so he could spend his retirement sitting in the lotus position and having students line up to meet him. In its simplest definition, *guru* means "teacher," and he humbly feels he has something to share. He is writing for everyone who feels disconnected or overwhelmed and who is yearning to be whole but who can't leave their nine-to-five or attend a weeklong spiritual retreat. Chick doesn't care that there are already a gazillion spiritual self-help books on the market. This one's different.

He says: "I hope my journey and hard-earned insights through the course of a normal, unextraordinary life will help you realize how extraordinary your 'ordinary' life really is. The greatest miracle is to be alive, to be here, experiencing this thing we call life."

And if that doesn't work out, well, Chick has just developed some nice two-bedroom condos on Lake Hopatcong in New Jersey that he can speak to you about.

JOE KITA
NOVEMBER 2, 2022

*Invite the truth of death into your life
earlier, and you'll receive its lessons.*

—B. J. MILLER, PALLIATIVE
PHYSICIAN AND AUTHOR

■　■　■

*There is no escaping the tragedy of life,
which is that we are all aging
from the day we are born.*

—FROM *BEING MORTAL* BY DR. ATUL GAWANDE

First Awakening:

I Am Not Immortal

I'M GOING TO BEGIN AT THE END, or rather what I once thought was the end.

I was eight or nine years old—a typical happy and carefree kid. Every summer from the time I was six, my parents would send my brothers and me away to camp. It is a tradition that persists among many Jewish families to this day. On July 1, which also happened to be my birthday, Mom and Dad would drive us to the train station in New York City, we'd say our goodbyes, and we kids would board the train for New York's Hudson Valley. Two hours later, we'd arrive at Camp Scatico, where we'd spend the next eight weeks.

Camp Scatico is a beautiful place, set on 275 wooded acres alongside two lakes. It was coed, with about 130 boys on one side and 130 girls on the other. Everyone lived in basic bunkhouses—simple rough-wood structures with no air-conditioning. You brought a little fan to cool yourself at night, but it could still get very hot.

I loved summer camp. I've always been into sports, and there was basketball, swimming, tennis, baseball, riflery, archery, and wonderful games like steal the flag and hounds and hares. Plus, there were arts and crafts and nature outings of all kinds. At the sound of reveille, I'd jump out of bed each morning with happy anticipation for the day.

But I was also a sensitive kid, prone to worry. And I had a temper. Sometimes when things didn't go my way, I would say, "I'm leaving!" I'd just walk out of camp. I was very headstrong. My two older brothers—thank God they were there—would hear their names over the camp loudspeaker: "Would Jack and Dick Atkins please come to the administration shack. Chick ran off into the woods again and won't come out."

They'd eventually settle me down, and I'd go back to enjoying everything the camp had to offer. In retrospect, those days in the Hudson Valley were some of the happiest days of my life.

But the nights there were a different story.

For some reason when I'd be lying in my bunk late at night, a singular thought would come to me:

I'm going to die. All this will continue for eternity without me in it.

And my brothers, my friends, Mom and Dad—everyone I love will die one day too.

It was a terrifying realization for a child so young and a long way from home. At night, surrounded by forest, there was nowhere to run. I'd just lie there with eyes wide, heart pounding, and my little fan struggling to stem the sweat.

Where this thought came from, I still don't know. No one close to me had died, nor was anyone even sick. I had never been to a funeral or a hospital, and other than the usual mishaps and scrapes from growing up, I had never been seriously injured myself. Like I said, I was generally a happy and carefree kid.

But when the lights went out, I'd start to fret. Worry and sadness would overcome me as these thoughts of death took over my mind. And the dichotomy of my days compounded these feelings. All the fun stuff I experienced during the day—all the excitement and joy—made the nights that much more unbearable because I realized it was all going to end.

Fortunately, this realization did not paralyze me or turn me into a morose introvert who nobody wanted to play with. It didn't cause me to think that something might be wrong with me, nor did I suddenly begin pestering my brothers or the camp counselors with questions about death. I pretty much forgot about it as soon as the sun came up. Any fear that lingered, I kept to myself. And I did a good job. If you had met me back then, you would never have suspected so many of my nights were sleepless.

But this realization did change me. From that moment forward, I became a worrier and, more important, a seeker of answers. Every child realizes their mortality at some point, but for me it had a greater impact. Once the initial fear wore off, I began asking myself these questions:

What is really going on?

Why are we here?

Does life have meaning?

Why must we die?

Am I and everyone I love just destined to disappear?

As I mentioned, my family was Jewish. But I didn't find any answers to these questions in religion. We were secular Jews, meaning we belonged to a temple and went to synagogue, but only on the High Holy Days (Rosh Hashanah and Yom Kippur). Like all good Jewish boys and girls, my brothers and I also attended Hebrew school twice a week in the afternoons. But other than that, religion wasn't a big thing in our family.

In fact, I remember being at synagogue, listening to the rabbi talking about the teachings of the Torah, and thinking in my young mind, *Well, how does he know that's true?* For example, we were taught that Jews are God's chosen people, and that He brought plagues upon the Egyptians and parted the Red Sea for the Jews. But He also let six million Jews die during World War II and permits thousands of children to starve to death daily in the world. I simply couldn't understand how people believed in this separate Being, this God who favored some people over others. Or why each organized religion insisted that its version of the truth was the correct one and that all other versions were wrong. This was my introduction to the problems created when people try to institutionalize truth, when they attempt to reduce the miracle and mystery of existence to a set of concepts.

So, I didn't find the answers I was looking for in Judaism, but it started me on a lifelong journey of exploration. My camp nightmare eventually became a dream of reaching a deeper understanding of who I am and why I'm here.

In my opinion, to be "religious" is not how it's defined today—as believing that God gave Moses a set of tablets, or that Jesus Christ was the son of God who was born in a virgin birth and was resurrected after death. Those, and the multitude of stories like them, are myths, parables of learning—pointers toward an understanding of deeper truths. We can be fed these stories as children and swallow them whole and believe, absolutely, that they're true. This is the case with hundreds of millions of people today. The problem arises when your truth contradicts someone else's truth, with each of you believing you are 100 percent right. To be religious is better defined as the search for meaning and for answers to life's deepest questions. I prefer to think of it as a spiritual quest.

And that's been my journey. When the realization of death hit me in that bunkhouse decades ago, I couldn't handle it emotionally. I was too young. All I saw was the reality of life being taken away. I'd like to say, after all these years of searching, that I now know what comes after death. But I don't. Different religions have different stories of heaven, hell, reincarnation, etc., but no one really knows. If somebody dead comes back and tells me directly, then I'll change my tune. But for now, it remains a mystery.

I know nothing about God. You can invent, pretend: I have a horror of pretending. If I do not know, I do not know.
—JIDDU KRISHNAMURTI

And all these years later, I still think about death every day. It no longer keeps me up at night, but it remains a steady presence in my life. Sometimes it makes me sad to think about everything I'll lose, but other times it makes me tremendously grateful for everything I have. Yes, *I'm going to die*, but I'm okay with that.

Years ago, after our morning game of tennis, I was chatting with a pastor friend of mine named Frank—just small talk about our plans for the day. He said he was going to preside over a funeral, mentioned something about the person who had died, and then added that he'd probably talk about how death should make us cherish life. And then he said, almost as an afterthought, "Yeah, but who really thinks about dying anyway?"

And I said, "Frank, I think about death every day."

"Really?" he replied.

"Yeah, I think about life and death on a daily basis."

We went on to have many deep philosophical conversations about death—his being what I'd call a true believer in his religious traditions, and my being a big questioner of those ideas. He used to say to me, "Chick, I really don't know anyone who thinks about death every day. And even if that's the case, most people would never admit to it."

There's a Latin phrase *memento mori*. It translates as "remember you are dying." Some orders of monks use it as a greeting. Their philosophy is that the meaning of life lies in the recognition of death. The more conscious we are of our impermanence, the more appreciative we become of living. Impermanence is also an important Buddhist contemplation.

I agree and identify with this way of thinking. It resonates with me. One of the main teachings of the Buddha is that every human eventually faces illness, old age, and death. To recognize this marks a beautiful widening of perspective. It makes us grateful. It makes us better people.

That being said, am I encouraging you to think about death on a daily basis? Not necessarily. There's no one right way to live for everyone. That's a very strong belief of mine, and it will echo through this book. We all have very different personalities. Some people are naturally happier, while others tend to be more depressed. There's a wonderful saying that's attributed to the Spanish poet Antonio Machado:

Travelers, there is no path; paths are made by walking.

It's fine to be inspired by other people's ideas, but to really live an awakened and enlightened life, we must realize we don't have to imitate anyone. Our essential natures are all the same, but our personalities are unique. There is no one path, only our path.

There's a classic Jewish story about a great rabbi named Reb Zusha. He was lying on his deathbed, upset. A student of his asked,

"Rebbe, why are you so sad? After all the great things you have accomplished, your place in heaven is assured!"

"I'm afraid," Zusha replied, "because when I get to heaven, God won't ask me, 'Why weren't you more like Moses?' or 'Why weren't you more like King David?' God will ask, 'Zusha, why weren't you more like Zusha?' And then what will I say?"

This story raises another point—the point of this book, really—and that is the importance of self-inquiry to learn who we really are and discover our true nature. The search that sprang from the realization *I'm going to die* was not just for an explanation of death but also for an understanding of this thing called *me* that I feared would die. It was the start of a search for my *true self.*

The great Korean Zen Master Seung Sahn explained it this way:

> But what is your true self? Your body has life and death. But your true self has no life, no death. You think "My body is me." This is not correct. This is crazy. You must wake up! I ask you, what are you? Where are you coming from? What is your name? How old are you? When you die, where will you go? These are all simple questions. Maybe you say, "My name is Robert." That is your body's name. What is your true self's name? Maybe you say, "I am 35 years old." But that is your body's age. What is your true age? Tell me, tell me!

From a young age, being completely identified with my body made me constantly fearful of death, sometimes overtly but more frequently at a level just below the surface of consciousness. At the very beginning of life, we are not identified with our bodies. This notion of a "me" in this body and a world out there I'm separate from has not formed. There is only a tremendous wonder and awe at the display of aliveness everywhere. But from the moment of communication, the reinforcement of this idea begins. "What a beautiful baby you are, look at those gorgeous blue eyes! You are Chick, I am Mommy, and this is Daddy." And this continues until the notion of separate people is so ingrained it's never questioned.

It is possible to wake up from this complete identification with the body as "me." Any number of things can happen to the body: we can lose hair or limbs, even have numerous organ removals or transplants, and yet the sense of "me-ness" doesn't change one iota. This should be our first clue that what we think of as "me" is not really the body, even though there is an intimate relationship with it. Our challenge is to discover the "me-ness" that is unchanging and not body- or time-bound.

So, when looked at in this way, death is not the opposite of life. Death is the opposite of birth. Life includes both birth and death. Birth and death are events, whereas life is the totality of experience. Life includes all events, all experiences. There is no point of separation between the experiencer, what we call "me," and the experienced, or "life." We are merely one of the myriad manifestations of life in its eternal movement.

I apologize if I've drifted into the deep end a bit. One of my goals for this book is to write in a straightforward way so you can understand and apply these philosophies to your everyday life, if you want. I intend to fully explore the concepts of separateness and consciousness later in the book, so don't worry if you don't fully grasp them now. Here's another story that might make it all clearer:

My mother died when she was in her eighties, and she had a big fear of death. One day I asked her, "Mom, what is it that you think you are that is going to die?"

She looked at me, puzzled, and said, "I don't really know. My body, I guess."

"Well," I replied, "what if I could prove to you that you are not your body?"

She nodded, interested.

"Remember when Nan died?" I continued. "We were both in the room. When she died, you immediately knew she was gone, even though her body was still lying there in front of us. So, you are not your body. It's your body that will die, not you."

I like to think that provided her with some solace. Since then, I've lost my father and my eldest brother, and viewing death in this way has helped me deal with their passings. Call it whatever you want—consciousness, life force, the Self ... it does not die. There is no Where for it to go.

It has taken me quite a bit of time and study to realize this. When I was younger, I was very much a materialist. I believed the scientists who said consciousness is born from the normal workings of the brain, from a mixture of atoms and nerve responses. For much of my life, that seemed pretty factual to me. But the realization and recognition of one's true nature changes that. The idea that there was nothingness, and then the big bang, and then suddenly there was everything also stopped making sense to me. In fact, it seemed backward. Consciousness, life, had to come first. The very notions of time and space are understood to be a concept within the eternal Now, the eternal Consciousness.

Time is an illusion.
—ALBERT EINSTEIN

And the "me" we experience in every moment is that Consciousness. It starts to sound a lot like God, doesn't it? But it's God without all the mythologies and dogmas that organized religion attach.

Typically, we go through our lives without examining for ourselves the nature of life, the deep fabric of existence and its meaning. It never seems important enough or crucial to what is happening at the moment. And if we are truly engaged with what is happening in the moment, wonderful. But if we start to become aware of the frequent feelings of dissatisfaction and dis-ease that accompany us throughout the day, the idea may arise to look a little deeper than what is happening in our external situation for the root cause of the feelings. The deeper we look, the deeper the cause appears to lie. Deep existential feelings of loneliness, separation, and fear are discovered. What is the cause? Where does this come from?

Regardless of your background, for many people there comes a point in life when the desire for deeper understanding and meaning becomes paramount. It may seem an innate pull, as it was for me from a young age, or it may result from later unhappiness and suffering. This can be a wonderful event, a beginning of the possibility of wisdom, of loosening the complete identification with your body and its story (or society's story for it)—an opening of the possibility of a revolution in consciousness.

It is my hope that this book will help you reach that wonderful event—that from your dark night in the woods, from what may seem like the end, will come a realization, or at least the inkling of an ambition to learn.

This will be your first awakening.

This will be your beginning.

What other people think of me
is none of my business.

—HEARD OFTEN AT ALCOHOLICS
ANONYMOUS MEETINGS

Second Awakening:

I Don't Need Your Approval

I WAS A STRAIGHT-A STUDENT all through high school—always near the top of my class. I knew what my parents and teachers wanted, and I delivered. But back in the rebellious 1960s and early '70s, excelling in school wasn't such a positive thing among kids. In fact, I used to hide my report card because I was embarrassed.

Good grades just weren't cool.

And neither was I—or at least not as cool as I wanted to be.

This was especially true around girls. I had always been naturally shy, plus I didn't have any sisters to teach me the ways of women. Camp Scatico occasionally organized socials where the boys and girls got to mingle. One night, I somehow managed to convince this cute girl to come out on the driving range with me. (That was the thing to do if you wanted to get lucky.) But I was so shy and afraid of being rejected that I didn't do anything. Obviously, she must have liked me, or she wouldn't have agreed to go along, but I just couldn't make the move. In fact, I didn't even know what "the move" was. My social awkwardness persisted all the way through high school and into college.

When I arrived at the University of Virginia, I knew I needed to break out, to be cool, so I joined the Phi Gamma Delta fraternity, or Fiji House, as it's more commonly known. Back then, Fiji had the reputation of being a party house, and my chapter certainly lived up to that.

This is all background to illustrate how the last thing I was looking for at college was any sort of spiritual realization or awakening. I was still a kid with a lot of questions, but I was primarily just out to have fun.

When I was a sophomore, I signed up for a class called Principles of Rehabilitation Techniques. I was trying to get into the highly rated undergraduate business school (McIntire School of Commerce) and needed another class to fill my schedule. It dealt with enlightened companies that were hiring disabled people. To be honest, I had little interest in this topic, but I'd heard that the course was a gut, and so had the hundred-plus kids who showed up on the first day of class.

The professor was a liberal-minded hippie type who was fully aware of why most of us were there. But he turned out to be a great teacher. He used the class as a launchpad for wide-ranging discussions about life and philosophy. In one class, he went off on a tangent about the acclaimed psychologist Abraham Maslow and his hierarchy of needs. The concept is usually depicted as a pyramid with basic human needs at the bottom (food, water, warmth, rest, safety) and higher-level needs (self-actualization) at the top. Maslow's theory was that our basic needs must be met before we can advance through other levels of needs (belonging, love, esteem) and reach self-actualization.

I'd never heard the term "self-actualized" before, and I was instantly enthralled by this idea of fully realizing one's potential. As an example of what was possible, the professor assigned us a little book to read. It was called *The Man Who Tapped the Secrets of the Universe.* I'll never forget it. It was about this unbelievable man named Walter Russell. Despite being essentially uneducated, he went on to become an incredibly successful painter, sculptor, architect, scientist, and even figure skater. He was a Renaissance man living a self-actualized life. It just blew me away—the fact that it was possible for a human being to excel in so many diverse areas, while living so freely and fearlessly. I realized that with the proper mindset, my potential was equally limitless.

In retrospect, I clearly had some level of awakening while reading this book. I felt something come alive in me. What I wanted from life came into focus just a bit more. I got an inkling of rewards beyond a diploma, material gain, and career. And according to Russell's example, I didn't need anyone's approval to get there. I could make my own rules.

But awakenings are not always lightning strikes. Sometimes they're much more subtle, and their charge recedes and becomes dormant after the initial revelation. Sometimes you may not even be aware that you've been "awakened," just that your perception of life has shifted a bit.

That's what I experienced. My life had changed, but I didn't fully realize it. And I certainly wasn't ready for it. I was having way too much fun at the fraternity!

But these lessons from Principles of Rehabilitation Techniques stuck with me. That class turned out to be the most interesting one I had in four years of college.

In the years since, as I continued my spiritual journey, I've thought a lot about why that class affected me so strongly. I think it stemmed from my having two overriding personality traits at the time: (1) a need for approval, and (2) a feeling of inadequacy, of not being good enough as I am. These are two sides of the same coin, but I'll discuss approval first.

From an early age, we are rewarded for good behavior. When we drink all our milk, finish our dinner, pee in the toilet, or share our toys, we are rewarded with attention, praise, and the occasional treat. This happens thousands of times as we grow and develop. Miguel Ruiz, in his classic book *The Four Agreements*, put it this way:

> *That's how we learn as children. Children believe everything adults say. We agree with them, and our faith is so strong that the belief system controls our whole dream of life. We didn't choose these beliefs, and we may have rebelled against them, but we were not strong enough to win the rebellion.*
>
> *… Children are domesticated the same way that we domesticate a dog, a cat, or any other animal. In order to teach a dog we punish the dog and we give it rewards. We train our children whom we love so much the same way that we train any domesticated animal: with a system of punishment and reward. We are told "You're a good boy" or "You're a good girl" when we do what Mom and Dad want us to do. When we don't, we are "a bad girl" or "a bad boy."*

I was very good at this game. I knew how to get the desired pat on the head from authority figures such as my parents and teachers. And for a long time, I enjoyed the rewards this brought. Their attention and approval made me feel worthy and good. But eventually, starting with that class in college, I began wondering if approval was a drug that maybe I needed to get off.

Here's a passage from the book *Awareness* by the Jesuit priest and psychotherapist Anthony de Mello that explains what I'm getting at:

If you wish to understand control, think of a little child that is given a taste for drugs. As the drugs penetrate the body of the child, it becomes addicted; its whole being cries out for the drug. To be without the drug is so unbearable a torment that it seems preferable to die. Think of that image—the body has gotten addicted to the drug. Now this is exactly what your society did to you when you were born.... You were given a taste for the drugs called approval, attention, success, making it to the top, prestige, getting your name in the paper, power, being the boss.... Having a taste for these drugs, we became addicted and began to dread losing them. Recall the lack of control you felt, the terror at the prospect of failure or of making mistakes, at the prospect of criticism by others. So you became cravenly dependent on others, and you lost your freedom. Others now have the power to make you happy or miserable. You crave your drugs, but as much as you hate the suffering that this involves, you find yourself completely helpless. There is never a minute when, consciously or unconsciously, you are not aware of or attuned to the reactions of others, marching to the beat of their drums. A nice definition of an awakened person: A person who no longer marches to the drums of society, a person who dances to the tune of the music that springs up from within.

The child that de Mello is describing was me. It's not that I had a bad childhood or that my mother and father were poor parents. Quite the contrary. I was a typical kid (give or take a few insecurities) raised in the typical manner. And therein lies the problem—and the challenge. Like just about everyone else (you, too, I'd guess), I became addicted to the drugs of approval and others' validation of me. I needed their smiles and nods and applause to feel valued and worthwhile. And when I didn't get that acknowledgment, for whatever reason, I felt rejected and inadequate.

Inadequacy. Here is the other side of that tarnished coin. Because I was addicted to approval, because I lived to please others, I let them set the standards by which I was judged and ultimately rewarded. I surrendered control of my young life. And as I constantly strove to satisfy other people, I became more and more dissatisfied with myself. My sensitive nature led to feelings of inadequacy and a near-constant fear of rejection if I fell short of those standards. I lived in quiet dread of not being good enough.

You can imagine the stress this puts one under. But again, I was not unique. This is what our children face. No wonder teens are so troubled. My feelings of inadequacy as a young man were the direct result of me having given the power of determining my worthiness to other people, whether they were teachers, colleagues, or even girls I wanted to date. And, unfortunately, this is the natural order of things.

For me, getting an inkling of the alternative didn't make me drop out of college or completely disrupt my life, as happened to many rebellious kids at the time. In the late 1960s, many American college kids, including many Jews, such as Jack Kornfield, Joseph Goldstein, Sharon Salzberg, Lama Surya Das (i.e., Jeff Miller), left and went east to search for truth and meaning. Thank God they did, as the collective wisdom they and others have brought to Western spirituality and society has been invaluable.

Like I said, what sparks an awakening can take time to become a flame. But the fire had been set within me. I now had a sense that true peace and happiness derive from our internal perspectives, beliefs, and thinking, not from outside events, like we normally assume in Western society.

Years later, I read an essay by Daniel Greenberg, the founder of Sudbury Valley School (a self-governing school in Massachusetts), where he called himself a "recovering A-student." I instantly thought, *That's me!* But grades are a yardstick of approval, nothing more. All the work and effort and anguish that went into striving for good ones—was it really for my benefit or for others? I thought of Walter Russell, the man who had supposedly tapped into the power of the universe. He had left traditional education at age nine.

Today I am a successful real estate developer in New Jersey. I'm a principal in the family company that my father founded in 1949. I've had the good fortune to become moderately wealthy, travel the world, and enjoy the many fruits of society's approval of me and my work. So, you're probably wondering how I came to balance the desire for personal independence with the attention and approval needed to succeed in this world.

But we do not need anyone's approval to be successful.

To better understand this statement, let's look at two words that are often used to describe the relationships we have with other people:

Dependence

Interdependence

These words are similar, but they are quite different. To live an awakened life, we need to sort these two ideas out. As we've seen, seeking other people's approval is being *dependent* on them for our happiness. But we don't live solitary lives. Realistically, most of us can't just say "I don't need anybody!" and go off to live in the woods. We live in an *interdependent* human society. We need other people, such as farmers, airline pilots, road builders, auto mechanics, and plumbers to do things that we cannot do by ourselves with any measure of skill.

And in exchange for these services, we give our skills and talents back to society.

Inter-dependence, of course, is a fundamental law of nature. Not only higher forms of life but also many of the smallest insects are social beings who, without any religion, law or education, survive by mutual cooperation based on an innate recognition of their interconnectedness.
—THE DALAI LAMA

Our parents cared for us at a time when we were too young to care for ourselves. We can acknowledge and be grateful for all that others do that enhances and enriches our lives. That's not the same as seeking their approval and giving them control over our inner feelings of peace and happiness. It's possible to be independent of other people's opinions and expectations of you while still being inter-dependent with them.

On a personal level, I am very grateful for the business path my father set, which allowed me to pursue my career with him as a role model and mentor. I had to sort out, however, that acknowledging his help and guidance didn't mean spending my life continuously looking for his approval. Many of us can never quite separate the two, having appreciation for what our parents did for us as opposed to looking for their approval as we grow into adulthood and maturity.

To be free from dependence involves being comfortable in your own moral authority. For much of my life, if somebody criticized me, I'd instantly feel terrible. I'd assume they were right and apologize, because I had given them power over my emotions and thoughts.

But now, when that sort of thing happens, I stop and think, *Are they right? Do I agree with them? Maybe I am responsible, and what I did was wrong or hurtful, and I should apologize. But maybe I'm not; maybe this is their stuff, and I don't have to accept that.* Either way, I'm the one who gets to choose. I'm living free from needing approval. I'm in control of my happiness and well-being. My happiness is my responsibility, not my wife's, my children's, or anyone else's. And their happiness is their responsibility.

What other people say about us, or think about us, has nothing to do with us.

Again, Miguel Ruiz from *The Four Agreements*:

> *What causes you to be trapped is what we call personal importance. Personal importance, or taking things personally, is the maximum expression of selfishness because we make the assumption that everything is about "me."*
>
> *… Nothing other people do is because of you. It is because of themselves. All people live in their own dream, in their own mind; they are in a completely different world from the one we live in.*
>
> *… Even when a situation seems so personal, even if others insult you directly, it has nothing to do with you. What they say, what they do, and the opinions they give are according to the agreements they have in their own minds. Their point of view comes from all the programming they received during domestication.*

It's not that we should remove the guardrails of moral behavior and do as we please. No, we should continue to act morally, to care about and respect other people. But don't do it out of some expectation of approval or reward; do it for the pure joy and satisfaction of doing it for yourself. I treat people well and with respect in business because *I want to*. I care about what is best for all involved, including myself. **There comes a point where the line should blur between "I'm doing this for me" and "I'm doing this for others."** Indeed, the problem with much of what passes as charity these days is that it's done so other people think well of us. A lot of times it's for self-aggrandizement. True charity seeks nothing in return. You do it because it feels right and you want to.

Choosing to live in an interdependent rather than a dependent world is the first step to becoming not only a useful, functioning, and compassionate member of society but also a happy, peaceful, and well-balanced individual.

To me, this is such a simple and foundational precept for success that I find it hard to believe it is not more widely practiced. I used to get into arguments with one of my college business professors who insisted that the way to get ahead is by stepping on other people— sort of using them as rungs in your ladder. This is what he taught his students! I used to tell him, "You're kidding me. That's wrong!" He got a big kick out of my attitude. Sadly, too much of Western capitalism has adopted this strategy. Unmitigated greed has become an accepted way of doing business.

What is it within us that becomes so addicted to attention and approval that it leads to such blind ambition and disregard for other human beings? What is it exactly that yearns for these drugs but is destined to never ultimately be satisfied by them?

The answer is what we call the *ego*.

I am an egomaniac with an inferiority complex.
—DESCRIPTION OFTEN HEARD IN
ALCOHOLICS ANONYMOUS MEETINGS

Ego is your sense of self-esteem or self-importance. It is your inner story about who you are, and it is the only thing that needs to be defended and protected from the criticism of others. But here's the thing: it's not real. Whether these feelings are building us up with arrogance and pride or tearing us down with criticism and self-loathing or fluctuating between the two, they are no more than passing thoughts and emotions.

To accept this fact, however, would mean the ego denying its own existence. So, it's naturally going to fight you tooth and nail. But try to keep an open mind.

In those first moments after you and I were born and before our parents gave us a name, we existed. Our brains weren't cognitively developed, but we were conscious, and we were *here*. That Being, even though it didn't have a name or much brain function, is our true essence, our true self. What happens, quite naturally, is that parents and society see this Being as a blank canvas. In all the ways we've already discussed, they paint it with the brush of separateness and feed it with approval or disapproval. And as the newborn is nourished and grows, so, too, does its ego. We live so closely with our egos that we eventually no longer see any separation between them and us. But your ego is not you. At best, it is a poor avatar of your true self.

So, how does one begin to dismantle the ego and get reacquainted with one's true essence? Just discussing and thinking about the situation is the first baby step—the raising of awareness. When we're criticized or rejected, it is the ego that feels hurt and causes subsequent suffering. But if we keep in mind that the ego does not really exist—that it is merely a mental construct—then there is nothing that needs defending. Criticism or not living up to expectations won't kill us. Let the immediate threat pass, and watch what happens.

Nothing.

You, or your true self, will still be here.

It will not feel offended or diminished. It will still feel just as it always has—at birth as it is now—*peaceful and whole.*

---

*Sticks and stones can break my bones,
but names can never hurt me.*

*The Golden Rule: Treat others as you
would like others to treat you.*

It really is true that most of what we need to know we learned in kindergarten but forgot with time and conditioning. The next time someone criticizes you, or the next time you don't get what you feel you're entitled to, pause for a moment and realize that *you* have the power to control what happens next. You can let your ego feel all righteous and offended and then get angry or sink into a funk that you're probably already way too familiar with. In other words, you can react the same way you've been reacting your entire life. Or *you* can decide that for this one time, you're not going to let this bother you. You're going to shrug it off because in the grand scheme of things, it really doesn't matter. What you'll find with this approach is that you've put a pin into the balloon that is your ego. It may not burst, but it will deflate, if only a little. And you'll begin to see that not only have you been emotionally controlled by other people but you've also surrendered control of your life and happiness to your ego.

This can be an empowering, if not life-changing, realization. The ability to live a free and fearless life without needing the approval of anyone, including your own ego, is one of the most important things we can achieve—the self-actualization referred to earlier. It is still possible to continue to seek career success, meaningful relationships, and material gain while understanding that none of that will provide lasting contentment unless we look at how our beliefs and thinking color our experiences.

Just consider how we normally communicate with each other. We do so as victims. We believe we're a victim of the boss, our spouse, our government, or whatever circumstances we find ourselves in. And we constantly commiserate with each other about being victims. Ask yourself how often this is the main topic at your coffeehouse or dinner table. Getting rid of the egotistic thinking that feeds this will help free yourself.

Doubt is not the opposite of faith;
doubt is an element of faith.

—PAUL TILLICH, CHRISTIAN THEOLOGIST

■ ■ ■

A heretic is a man who sees with his own eyes.

—GOTTHOLD EPHRAIM LESSING,
GERMAN PHILOSOPHER

Third Awakening:

Others Think like Me; I'm Not Crazy!

IT HAD BEEN A WILD NIGHT. I'd been out late partying, and when I got back to my friend's apartment, I couldn't fall asleep. My mind was racing, and I was babbling about all sorts of things. At one point, my best friend, Steve, tossed me a book and said, "Hey, read this, I think you'll like it."

I looked at the cover, and it was this old Indian guy with a long name I couldn't pronounce.

"No offense, but I don't want to read some Indian guru," I replied.

"Just try it," he insisted. "I couldn't understand it, but I think you will."

So, I started reading, and I was immediately struck by how plain spoken the author was. It wasn't what I had expected. He was saying that he wasn't interested in what I'd read or been taught. He didn't care what the Bible or the Upanishads or other holy books said, or even what Jesus or the Buddha preached. Instead he stated that we're here; it is now; we are human beings who are suffering; let's explore together and discover what's real and true.

I instantly identified with this. All those times in Hebrew school and at temple when the rabbi was going on about God parting the Red Sea for Moses or sending his death angel to kill the firstborn sons of Egypt, those stories never meant anything to me. They were fairy tales, myths from long ago that were unrelatable to my life. They portrayed God as all knowing and loving, but someone who still needed to be obeyed and feared. Now here was this famous guy who was respected worldwide giving voice to the same stuff that was in my head. I couldn't believe it. There was this explosion in me. In fact, I'm getting chills now as I remember it, even though nearly fifty years have passed.

I stayed up until dawn reading that book. It was called *The Only Revolution*, and it was written by J. Krishnamurti. I became obsessed with him and set out to read everything he'd ever written or that had been written about him. I wanted to know everything.

His story turned out to be fascinating. Born in India in 1895, he was "discovered" by a purported clairvoyant with the Theosophical Society, who said the boy had "the most wonderful aura he'd ever seen." The young Krishnamurti was removed by this group from his family and nurtured, educated, and groomed to be the next World Teacher—a spiritual entity who would guide humankind to the next level. His reputation as the new messiah grew through the early 1900s as he traveled and spoke around the world. But in 1929, after his own series of awakenings, he broke with Theosophy and its grand plan for him, stating,

> *I maintain that truth is a pathless land, and you cannot approach it by any path whatsoever, by any religion, by any*

sect ... The moment you follow someone you cease to follow the Truth ... I am concerning myself with only one essential thing: to set man free. I desire to free him from all cages, from all fears.

Wow. Reading Krishnamurti was a revelation and a relief for me. Here was a spiritual sage saying what had been roiling around in my brain for years. He had the courage, the fearlessness, to stand up and declare that none of what was being passed around as truth was necessarily true. Furthermore, the fact that hundreds of millions of people insisted it was true still didn't make it true. This gave me the sense that I wasn't crazy. It validated my skepticism and set the way for my inner journey.

It changed my life immediately.

But it didn't change my life *outwardly*. By all appearances I was still the same guy I'd always been. I behaved in the same ways. I had recently graduated from the University of Virginia and was working in the real estate development business with my father and older brother. My father had started the business in the early 1950s after serving in World War II. What began as a home-building business supported by Veterans Administration loans expanded into a commercial real estate company encompassing residential projects and office buildings.

So, during the week I worked diligently at learning about real estate, but on the weekends I chased the good times with sex, drugs, and rock and roll. One of my favorite haunts, the Lone Star Cafe in Greenwich Village, had a fifty-foot lizard on the roof and a motto above the door that read "Too Much Ain't Enough." I took that to heart in those days. And it worked pretty darn well, until it didn't, which is a story for a later chapter.

All of that remained the same. But *inwardly* I was slowly becoming a different person.

Happiness is your nature; it is not wrong to desire it.
What is wrong is seeking it outside when it is inside.
—RAMANA MAHARSHI, INDIAN HINDU SAGE

The tiny flame inside that had been lit by the possibility of psychological liberation, of self-actualization, became a little brighter. Reading Krishnamurti validated the skepticism about religion and truth that I had been carrying deep inside me for years. It was a huge realization on my spiritual path—a validation of my curiosity and wonder about *What's going on here?*

Years later, I read an excellent essay by the spiritual teacher Joan Tollifson. Here's an excerpt:

> *Science handles human curiosity and the desire for answers in an excellent way, while belief-based religion and spirituality are prone to handling it in the worst possible way. The scientific method is based on testing things out, actually trying to disprove rather than prove a hypothesis—and if it holds up to all that scrutiny, then it becomes a working theory, like the theory of evolution, but even then, theories are always open to being proven wrong.*
>
> *Religion, on the other hand, when it is based on belief, regards its ideas as Truths that cannot be questioned. In many cases, these Truths are believed to have been revealed by God. They are considered infallible and of divine origin. This leads easily to dogmatism, fundamentalism, fanaticism, magical thinking, gullibility, exploitation, holy wars, crusades, witch burnings, and generally lots of suffering.*

But at its best, religion is not about belief. It is about direct experiencing and a devotion to the aliveness of this moment, here and now. It involves a direct exploration of the living actuality.

Science without religion is lame.
Religion without science is blind.

—ALBERT EINSTEIN

There is a difference, however, between being skeptical and being cynical. Skepticism involves questioning accepted facts and opinion. Ideas are approached with open-mindedness, curiosity, and wonder. They are also screened with logic and rationality. Shedding fear of other's opinions is key, being willing to stand one's ground alone. It is our antidote to blind faith. Faith that all is fundamentally well is wonderful, but it should not be blind; it should be a clear vision that life is a miracle in ways we cannot grasp with even the greatest logic and rationality. What is lost today in much spirituality is that this doesn't mean we toss logic and rationality out the window. We learn to rationally understand the limits of rational thought.

Cynicism, however, may appear grounded in logic and rationality, but it is in fact grounded in an emotional state of despair caused by loss of hope and faith in any goodness of humanity. It lies in the belief that people are solely motivated by their own self-interest. The cynic distrusts everyone and automatically questions their motives. Cynicism leads to narrow-mindedness, anger, and fear.

I'm not just skeptical about what other people say; I've also become skeptical about what *I think*. Miguel Ruiz, in his book *The*

Voice of Knowledge, encourages us to adopt two rules that will change our lives: (1) don't believe yourself, and (2) don't believe anybody else.

You may call it thinking, but I call it the liar
that lives in my head.
—MIGUEL RUIZ

Nothing that I say is true.
—ADYASHANTI, AMERICAN SPIRITUAL TEACHER

It's the ego we spoke about earlier—this avatar of ourselves that we've created whose only job is to defend its existence. And it will lie and cheat and deceive to do so.

That's because the truth cannot be spoken. It cannot be put into words. The description is not the thing; it can never, ever be what it is describing, no matter how beautiful or poetic the description. The recipe is not the meal: one cannot eat a recipe.

This is the reason Ruiz advises us not to believe anything anyone says or anything we think. All thoughts are conceptual and, therefore, not real or true. We may think they are beautiful words; ugly, revolting words; or anything in between, but they are just words, just thoughts, and empty of any reality other than being just words and thoughts.

The difference between great spiritual teachers and you and me is that they know they aren't speaking the truth; they know their thoughts and words are not true. They are *pointing* at the truth they are experiencing, but they don't confuse what they're saying with the truth they are describing. We do, with their words and with our thoughts. We think they are speaking the truth; we think that what we think is the truth. This is why we can't hear them; this is why we listen and listen and cannot see what they're pointing at. What they're pointing at is so simple and immediate that we can't see it because we are looking for the meaning in their words, which are empty of meaning in and of themselves.

Jesus always made a point in his teaching to begin with the phrase "The Kingdom of Heaven is like this ..." He was not, as most interpretations assert today, pointing at some future reality after we die. He was describing the state of mind that experiences the present moment as heaven, as living in the Garden of Eden. He consistently used the phrase "is like this" to make sure nobody confused his description with the reality he was pointing at. Unfortunately, the very thing he was worried about—people taking his words literally, worshipping his ideas and concepts as opposed to reality—is exactly what has happened in organized religion. It is what always happens when we try to institutionalize truth. The original meaning of the teaching is lost. Similarly, the biblical story of the Garden of Eden is misinterpreted as referring to some time period in the distant past, when in fact it is a parable about living each moment in a State of Being that is not defined by concepts. This is what eating from the Tree of Knowledge is referring to: it is a cautionary tale of losing touch with the miraculous nature of true reality by conceptualizing it.

Truth repeated is a lie.

—KRISHNAMURTI

What did Krishnamurti mean when he said this? I was fascinated by it and pondered the meaning for years. The deep meaning is this: When we experience the truth of something for ourselves, then we are no longer imitating or quoting anyone else; we are speaking our truth. When we are just repeating what someone else said, even someone held in high esteem, such as Buddha or Jesus, we are not speaking truth because we do not really know whether it is true or not for ourselves.

If you can't explain it to a six-year-old, then you don't understand it yourself.
—ALBERT EINSTEIN

This is a difficult concept to grasp. Indeed, most people never understand it, and that's one of the reasons why the world and so many people in it are suffering. The lies we're told and the lies we tell ourselves have led us away from the truth.

Here's another way of looking at this: Think of the ego as a dirty pane of glass through which we view ourselves and the world. It has become streaked and smudged from years of people putting their fingerprints on us. But we're just as complicit because we haven't bothered to clean it. In fact, the view still looks pretty good to us. We're unaware that we're not seeing clearly and that our perceptions are clouded. An awakening is like a window washing. Maybe it doesn't immediately eliminate all the grime, but it gets rid of a layer or two of ego through which the truth can better shine.

So how then do I—a sixtysomething Jewish real estate developer from New Jersey with a naturally opinionated and passionate personality (a college fraternity brother once said of me, "Chick will argue with anybody about anything at any time")—apply this thinking to my daily life? What are the practical applications for me and you? It's simple but not easy to do. However, through practice it can become habit. In business, in relationships, in even the most cursory interactions with other people, I am never married to my point of view. I maintain a healthy skepticism about what's being said and what's in my head.

There's a great scene in *Fiddler on the Roof* where Tevye comes upon two men having a vicious argument about a horse. One is insisting that the horse he bought is twelve years old, while the guy who sold it to him is swearing the horse is only six. One is demanding his money back while the other is insisting he did nothing wrong. Tevye listens to the first man and tells him he is right. Then he listens to the second man and tells him he is right. A third man, who had been looking on, says, "What are you talking about? They can't both be right." To which Tevye replies, "You're right too!"

I love that scene because it shows there are always different sides to a story. I'm very opinionated, I can be insistent and passionate, but I always try to be open to the other person's point of view. This informs all aspects of my life. I resist the dogmatic and let my skepticism come through.

So, maybe we find ourselves in a situation where I have a strong opinion and you have a strong opinion, where I want something and you want something different. After the arguing subsides, I look at the situation as an independent third party (as Tevye did) and try to be an objective judge—even of my own opinion. I try to take everybody's well-being into account, what's best for all concerned, including myself, and then make the best decision I can. It's a non-dogmatic approach to daily living that removes the ego and helps everyone involved get closer to the truth.

*If we want peace of mind, we need to give up
our job as general manager of the Universe.*

—LARRY EISENBERG, AUTHOR

■ ■ ■

*That the birds of worry and
care fly about your head
This you cannot change,
But that they build nests in your hair,
This you can prevent.*

—CHINESE PROVERB

Fourth Awakening:

I Worry Too Much

BY NOW I WAS IN MY LATE TWENTIES, recently married, and growing with the family business, which provided both income and security. Ellen and I had even bought a house. We closed on it less than a month before our wedding. We were in love, and we had our whole lives ahead of us.

Life was good.

But one night we were lying in bed, and I suddenly became conscious of what my mind was doing. It was looking for something to worry about! It was scanning my personal life and my work life and then the world situation until it found something to land on and stress about. At that moment, I realized how much this had been happening nightly and probably for many of my waking hours. It just hit me. The thought came powerfully into my head: *I'm driving myself nuts, and this is no way to live.*

Looking back, it was another awakening, the difference between knowing something intellectually (that I had a tendency to worry) and true insight (that this was causing much psychological suffering).

Unfortunately, this *is* the way most of us live. We are in an epidemic of anxiety, with negative psychological as well as physical effects. On one level a certain amount of worry is understandable, especially if you live in poverty or a war-torn country. One cannot tell someone who has bombs dropping all around them, or whose children do not have enough to eat, not to worry. But like me, you're probably not in that situation, yet we still lie awake worrying.

In 2019 researchers at Penn State University conducted a study in which they sent periodic text messages to a small group of undergraduates. These messages prompted them to record all their worries from the past two hours. In the next phase of the study, these same students reviewed their worry lists every evening for thirty days. The researchers had them focus on worries that could be tested during this period, such as "I hope I don't fail my exam," rather than "I'm going to die of a heart attack just like my father did."

Now here's the fascinating part: 91 percent of testable worries did not come true. And of the remaining 9 percent, the outcome was better than expected about a third of the time. For roughly one in four undergrads, *none* of their worries materialized. The researchers characterized these findings as "worry's deceit."

I've had a lot of worries in my life, most of which never happened.
—MARK TWAIN

The negative effects of anxiety and worry, both psychological and physical, are well documented. The stress that results has been scientifically linked to many chronic conditions, including heart disease, rheumatoid arthritis, and depression.

I have always been a worrier. It just seemed to be part of my natural resting state, and, over the years, I had come to accept this. It wasn't like I was an anxious person, although I know that sounds contradictory, but I was never paralyzed by worry or depressed by it. I was a relatively happy young man who, for some reason, had this level of unease about things running just below the surface of my consciousness. Then, in down moments, my mind would go to its default setting and begin ruminating obsessively.

That night when I was lying in bed with Ellen, I was probably worrying about work stuff and what was going on in the world. But I also remember wondering about why I was so lucky in my life situation when there was so much suffering and struggle for others. *Why is the world the way it is? Why are human beings the way they are? Why do we treat each other so badly? My life had always been pretty darn good, but I'm not any better or more deserving than anyone else. Why is that?* Thoughts like these genuinely troubled me.

That night was also no different from any other night. It was rare when I didn't either worry myself to sleep or wake up in the middle of the night fretting about something or other. But for some reason, this time I realized the psychological toll it was taking on me. The proverbial light bulb went on.

Why this realization came when it did—indeed, why any awakening occurs when it does—I have no idea. There is no clear answer to why revelations occasionally come to us, or why they strike some people and not others. It's as if the universe and all your personal experiences and musings coalesce for an instant, and we see things in a fresh way. Buddhism tells us there are ten thousand reasons for everything that happens, meaning there's an infinite number of causes. It's the interdependence we discussed previously. Small things matter, and we are all part of a bigger system. But our minds have a hard time accepting an explanation like this. Our minds want to simplify things, to settle on a cause for the effect. But the truth of the matter is we can never know.

What is worry anyway?

Worry can be defined simply as fear-based thinking. And when we believe our worries to be real, we create real consequences. We trigger an emotional reaction (anxiety/stress), which releases certain hormones that, over time, can lead to psychological and physical disease. The greater our level of worry and the more we attach to it (believing our thoughts about what's happening to be true), the greater the suffering we inflict on ourselves (and others).

Worry is just another form of fear. It can stem from feeling like we're not in control of a situation or from being unable to accept it. I feared death. I feared not being good enough. I feared having nonconformist beliefs. I feared worrying too much. Indeed, much of my behavior to this point in my life arose from unconscious patterns of belief—that I wasn't good enough as I am or that I couldn't accept the situation as it is.

But this was about to change. That night in bed, I experienced something that I had never experienced before, and it's key to stopping the runaway thought-train in our head that controls us. What had been operating under the surface of conscious perception was becoming clearer.

I had been reading for years about how we are not our thoughts. It's a fundamental assertion in all spiritual teachings. Essentially, it means that who (or what) we really are is separate from the mechanism that generates our thoughts. For example, we are having a conversation right now. I am expressing my opinions, and you are reading and considering them. But what is it that is having this experience? A thought can't experience anything; it's just a bit of energy arising in our brains (or wherever). What is having this experience is something deeper, something indescribable.

What turned this late-night experience into an awakening for me was that, for the first time in my life, I felt myself *observing* my thoughts. And in order to do that, you have to be separate from the content of experience.

Eckhart Tolle, in his book *The Power of Now*, outlines an easy way to experience this separateness. "*Close your eyes and say to yourself: 'I wonder what my next thought is going to be.' Then become very alert and wait for the next thought. Be like a cat watching a mouse hole. What thought is going to come out of the mouse hole?*"

As you wait, become aware of who (or what) is doing the waiting. That Being or Consciousness or whatever you want to call it is who (or what) you truly are. And that is what everyone else is as well, and indeed, the entire universe. Awakening is really just the recognition of this deep truth about the Witnessing Consciousness. I had never experienced this before, and frankly it was still many years before I understood it as I'm describing it now.

But again, it's not like I jumped out of bed and shook Ellen awake, so she could roll her eyes at me and tell me to go back to sleep. No, it was a startling but, at the same time, subtle revelation. In the same way, there was no explosion inside me as when I first read Krishnamurti. I woke up the next morning, showered, got dressed, and went to work just like I always did.

But I was different.

I was now aware that *I worry too much!* Not in the joking sense that most people make that statement, but on a much deeper, knowing level. And the source of all that worry and dread was my old nemesis, the ego. It had been haunting me yet again without my realizing it.

If your eyes are blinded with your worries, you cannot see the beauty of the sunset.
—KRISHNAMURTI

Our worries generally fall into two categories—either regretting the past or fretting about the future. This is what the ego is made of—either mulling over what's already been or ruminating about what might be. The ego recreates and creates scenarios that are nonexistent in the present. They exist only in the bygone past and a fictional future. So, what you're worrying about, what's keeping you up at night, is only in your mind. Your problems are not here now.

There will always be life situations to deal with; this is what it means to live. There are bills to pay, children get sick, governments change, etc. So we need to think about these things, plan our course of action, understand and work to achieve our goals. But that's not what's causing you pain. Go ahead and make your grocery list. Book the summer family vacation. Contribute to your 401(k). Vote in elections for the candidates you feel are best. That is showing up for your life and participating in society. By all means, continue doing that. But resist getting caught up in all the what-ifs surrounding those life situations. What if the supermarket is out of toilet paper again? What if our flight gets canceled? What if I die before retirement? What if so-and-so gets elected and the country descends into chaos? We bombard ourselves with these messages daily. But as those Penn State researchers found, 91 percent of the time none of your what-ifs will happen. This is the source of our psychological pain and suffering. Not what is actually happening, but the stories we tell ourselves in our minds about what is happening or may happen.

Byron Katie, another one of the great spiritual teachers of our time, says that awakening is very simple. Just realize that when you argue with reality, you lose, but only 100 percent of the time. Arguing with reality is the source of all your worry and anger. Yet 99.99 percent of us argue with reality all the time. I'm angry at my wife—behave like this so I can be happy! I'm upset at my children—do as I tell you so I can be happy! I've had it with the world—why can't things change so I can be happy! Anything we fill in after the phrase "I will be happy when _____" is an impediment to our inner peace and happiness.

When you really stop to consider the predicament we've gotten ourselves into, it can become quite humorous. Imagine, I would worry about worrying too much! Buddha said that if we just realize the way things are, we'll start laughing hysterically at all the needless suffering we've caused ourselves. The past and the future do not exist; they're just stories and thoughts. There is nothing other than the Now.

It is not, however, quite right to call what I'm referring to "the present moment," as so much pop literature does these days. It is greater than that. It is not a moment in time; it is outside of time. It's more accurate to describe it as "the eternal present." It is always here and accessible to all of us. The irony is that we cannot be anywhere else or experiencing anything other than the eternal present. Even when we are regretting the past or worrying about the future, we are still doing it in the eternal present.

I don't profess to not worry anymore. I still worry about my kids, what's happening at work, and the state of the world. But I don't get caught up in it; I no longer attach to it. I watch what's going on, and there is automatically some space between me, the experiencer, and what I see happening in my mind. I'm not suffering psychologically from worry the way I used to. Sure, I feel sad sometimes, especially when I dwell on the suffering of others. But I don't sink into despair and depression. I just watch my worries happen. It's like watching clouds float by in the sky. The sky is not scarred, stained, or damaged by the nature of the clouds arising and passing away within it. There can be a peace that comes while I'm doing this. I am conscious that my mind is contemplating things at the same time that I feel the deep peace of ever-present Consciousness.

The space I feel is not a barrier between myself and anxiety or stress. I don't like putting up barriers because that means I'm defending something. Allowing is a better description. Having space allows me to just be and to give compassion. Becoming familiar with the Observer or the Witness is to allow space for everything to come.

Here's a wonderful poem from the thirteenth-century poet and Islamic scholar Rumi that beautifully captures the openness that's required to find enlightenment. It's called "The Guest House."

This being human is a guest house.
Every morning a new arrival.

A joy, a depression, a meanness,
some momentary awareness comes
as an unexpected visitor.

Welcome and entertain them all!
Even if they're a crowd of sorrows,
who violently sweep your house
empty of its furniture,
still, treat each guest honorably.
He may be clearing you out
for some new delight.

The dark thought, the shame, the malice,
meet them at the door laughing,
and invite them in.

Be grateful for whoever comes,
because each has been sent
as a guide from beyond.

We are here, and it is now. Further than that, all human knowledge is moonshine.

—H. L. MENCKEN

■ ■ ■

Enlightenment is an accident; spiritual practice makes one accident prone.

—TRADITIONAL SPIRITUAL SAYING,
AUTHOR UNCERTAIN

Fifth Awakening:
I Should Try Meditation

IT'S ONE THING TO REALIZE that worry is causing me unnecessary distress and suffering. But it's another thing entirely to commit to doing something about it. Having grown up in the '60s with an interest in spirituality, I had heard about Transcendental Meditation, or TM. It was created by a bearded, white-robed Indian sage named Maharishi Mahesh Yogi. He traveled the world teaching people his technique of silent mantra meditation. When practiced for fifteen to twenty minutes twice daily, it was supposed to be the gateway to relaxed awareness, stress relief, and higher states of consciousness.

The Maharishi and TM were catapulted into the public eye (and got my attention) when the Beatles attended one of his lectures in the United Kingdom and then traveled to India to train at his ashram. Other celebrities were there, including Mike Love from the Beach Boys, Donovan, and the actress Mia Farrow. Whether anyone "transcended" is debatable, but it is reported that eighteen of the songs that eventually appeared on the Beatles' White Album were written there.

I was inspired and intrigued by this, and I tried to meditate a few times when I was in my teens and early twenties. I did it on my own, not going to any TM class or guru, just finding a quiet spot in the house, sitting down, assuming the fancy position, and waiting for something to happen. I thought maybe fireworks would go off, or lights and bells, and I'd suddenly be on the astral plane and see God. But nothing happened. It was just me sitting alone on the floor with my knees hurting and my mind bouncing all over the place like it normally did. So, I quickly concluded *I can't do this,* or *I don't know how to do this.* And I gave up and went back to living life and trying to have fun.

But I never forgot about meditation. It was always in the back of my mind on a sort of subconscious bucket list. So, after awakening to the fact that worry was running (and ruining) my life and deciding to finally try to do something about that, it was natural for me to return to this thing—whatever it was—that was supposed to help me live in the now.

Remember my friend Steve, who gave me Krishnamurti's book after a night of partying and insisted I read it? Well, his younger brother, Stew, gave me another book that changed my life. This one was *Everyday Zen* by Charlotte Joko Beck. It enabled me to see meditation in an entirely different way and start a practice that has persisted to this day.

Basically, she wrote that meditation is not about achieving some extraordinary state or experience. It's simply about showing up, sitting down, and being with everything as it is. If your mind is going a million miles a minute, notice that it's going a million miles a minute. If your knees hurt, notice that your knees hurt. If you're feeling bored, notice that you're feeling bored. That's how she defined meditating, and I had a very strong reaction when I read it. *Oh, I can do that. I can just sit and be with whatever comes up.* And so, I started doing that—and I have never really stopped. For me, it was that easy.

Comparing those two times—when I first tried meditating and then when I tried it again after reading *Everyday Zen*—I'd say the experiences were the same but my mind's reaction to the experiences was completely different. Let me explain what I mean by that because it relates to everything I'm trying to get across in this book.

Both experiences were the same—I was sitting quietly by myself—but in the first instance that wasn't acceptable to me because I expected something transcendental to happen. So, when nothing happened, I felt like a failure. But in the second instance, when I sat down with no expectation other than being with whatever came up, I felt I had succeeded. I did it!

Expectations are premeditated resentments.
—ALCOHOLICS ANONYMOUS SAYING

Think about how often we head into everyday life situations brimming with expectations. Work expectations, relationship expectations, vacation expectations, restaurant expectations … you name it. Now consider how infrequently those expectations are met and how you feel afterward—disappointed, frustrated, occasionally even angry or depressed. But it's not the situation that causes this—after all, it's just a situation or experience. Rather, it's your ego-centric expectations that cause you to feel these negative emotions and often bring suffering to yourself and others.

---

*There is nothing either good or bad
but thinking makes it so.*
—SHAKESPEARE'S HAMLET

What I say now may be difficult to swallow (even for me many times), but all situations or experiences are morally neutral within themselves. We add moral judgment to them based on the conditioning of our minds and psyches. We may try to add weight to our beliefs by saying it is not our morality, it is God's, but this is not true. You have decided what God likes and dislikes, based on your own beliefs or what you have read. If the idea of God is to have any meaning, it is in referring to the totality of Reality, the totality of things as they are, seen and unseen. There is no God dividing our lives into good and bad, Good and Evil, etc. Ultimately, there is no division of "things" in reality at all. Our mind divides the world into "this" and "that" and then decides which parts it likes and which it doesn't, which parts are acceptable and which aren't. This is the root cause of our personal suffering.

When I use the word God, I simply mean Reality as it is.
—BYRON KATIE, TEACHER/AUTHOR

To set up what you like against what you dislike is the disease of the mind ... Do not search for the truth; only cease to cherish opinions.
—SENG-T'SAN, THIRD CHINESE PATRIARCH OF ZEN

So, I was starting to meditate regularly, and I was really excited about it. I recall discussing this with Ellen at the time. I probably was going on about how all you needed to do was just be with everything as it is when she asked, "But how do you motivate yourself to do something where you don't know the result, or whether it will be what you want?" And I remember saying, "I guess you just have to have faith that something good will come."

And something good did come.

On one very basic level, I felt satisfaction. *I was meditating! I could do this after all!* But it went beyond that. As I sat there noticing my mind bouncing all over the place, not trying to control it or distract myself from it, just being with those thoughts as they randomly came and went, I started feeling peaceful. I didn't have to fight with my mind all the time, nor did I have to react to every idea that came into it; I could just observe it doing its thing, and I'd be fine. I could let any worry or bit of negativity arise that wanted to arise and be okay with it. It wouldn't preoccupy me or drag me down. In fact, after rising to the surface of my consciousness, these thoughts often evaporated just as quickly as they had appeared.

> *If you try to win the war with your mind,*
> *then you will be at war forever.*
> —FROM *TRUE MEDITATION* BY ADYASHANTI

And eventually, after meditating like this for a while, I started to feel empowered, like I could handle anything life delivered. All I needed was to sit and do this for a few minutes whenever I could. No pressure, no magic posture, no mantra, no observation of the breath (although observing the breath is a wonderful entry point into present-moment awareness), no rules, no expectations ... just allowing everything to be as it is—the good *and* the bad—and being fine with that.

Meditation is being willing to put down all doing so we can experience being. You've probably heard the old saying "We are human *beings,* not human *doings.*" Maybe you even have a T-shirt with that on it somewhere. But most people never really experience themselves as human *beings.* It's an incredibly fresh experience to put down doing. Meditation facilitates this. Meditation, in its simplest form, is doing nothing and letting whatever happens happen. If you're doing anything at all, it's noticing what's happening. It's a heightened state of perception. But it's not some extraordinary altered state of consciousness. Rather, it's our natural state, which is one of pure awareness.

> *The peace and stillness you're trying*
> *to attain is already here.*
> **—ADYASHANTI**

As I've said many times, I am not a guru. No one is ever going to mistake me for the Maharishi. I struggle daily with many of the same things you do. But I have learned over the years to use meditation to keep my struggles in perspective and minimize the suffering they cause myself and others.

I've found there is no "art" to meditation, no technique you must adhere to if you don't want to. Ellen now has a very good meditation practice of her own. She rises early in the morning, gets on her mat, and meditates. She's very disciplined. But you'll probably be surprised to learn that I don't have a daily practice like that anymore. Sometimes I just sit in the backyard and have a cigar and look at the trees, listen to the birds, or feel the breeze. Right now, as we're having this conversation, I can start meditating. I can become aware of my butt in the chair, my spine against the backrest, and my fingertips on the keyboard. Right this second, I hear a leaf blower outside my window, and I notice a bit of irritation arise at the disturbance. But I just relax and sink into everything that's happening. My awareness of what is here right now heightens, without me trying to control anything.

And although I've used the word "I" to describe my process, I am not really there, at least not in the way I normally think I exist. There is no separate thing hearing the birds or the leaf blower; it's just a *hearing* of the birds and the leaf blower.

That's meditation for me—when at any moment, I can step back, take a break, and *lose myself* in the moment.

Meditation is no longer as mystical or even as novel as it was when the Beatles traveled to India. It has been well researched in the decades since, and its benefits have been quantified by science. And there are many benefits, both physical and psychological. On its website, the Mayo Clinic lists ten ways meditation can improve emotional and physical well-being, including helping manage stress, improve sleep quality, and lower blood pressure and resting heart rate. Some studies suggest that meditation may have preventive qualities as well, helping us withstand disease and illness and remain healthier longer.

All this makes sense to me, but I can only attest to the personal rewards that I've enjoyed after years of meditating. I'm sixty-six years old, and I feel very healthy and young in heart and mind. I don't think that's solely due to meditation, because I exercise, watch what I eat, and do yoga regularly, but it has certainly played a role. My mind is noticeably calmer and quieter. I still worry, but not with the obsessiveness I used to. Overall, I believe meditation has contributed to making me a happier and more content and grateful individual. Maybe it has even helped make me more successful. Who knows?

There is a wonderful story and quote that's attributed to the Buddha: When asked what he gained from meditation, he supposedly laughed and said, "Nothing. However, let me tell you what I have lost: anger, depression, insecurity, fear of old age and death."

Whether the Buddha really said that or not is beside the point. Its truth goes far beyond whoever came up with it. I haven't really *gained* anything through meditation. My inherent nature—*your* inherent nature, *everyone's* inherent nature—is one of stillness and peace. These qualities become blocked or hidden by our anger, resentment, and worry but are always present behind the emotional turmoil, as the sun continues to shine behind the clouds.

> *There is no way to happiness and peace.*
> *Happiness and peace are the way.*
> —BUDDHA

We are all looking for peace and happiness. That's what we really want. Why do you want to get married and have kids? Peace and happiness. Why do you want more money? Peace and happiness. Why do you want a bigger house and a nicer car? Peace and happiness. Why do you want to be famous and have lots of Twitter followers? The same answer again and again and again. But why, if we contemplate this just a bit more, don't we go directly to the source? Instead of chasing all these intermediary things like sex, money, fame, and materialism and hoping they'll bring us what we're looking for, why not just seek out our natural state of peace and happiness?

> *If happiness were to be found where you've been*
> *looking, you would have found it a long time ago.*
> —CHERI HUBER, ZEN TEACHER

Obviously, it must be because we're either unaware that peace and happiness is our natural state or because we've been given the wrong directions for getting there. Meditation is essentially a goalless practice. It is not, as is commonly believed, about stopping our thinking. No one has ever been able to stop their thinking. What is possible is to start noticing the gap between thoughts, the spaces. There is gold in the spaces, the potential to notice that "I" am still here, without thought. What is this "I" that is here when thinking is not?

> *Before thinking, my mind, your mind,*
> *Buddha's mind, all the same.*
> **—ZEN MASTER SEUNG SAHN**

You don't have to get anywhere. All the peace and happiness you are looking for is already here. You just need to become aware of this fact. If there is a goal in meditation, it is to become aware of being aware. As this ability increases, we can learn to rest in awareness.

My meditative journey has largely been a positive one. But for some people it can be upsetting, especially at first. Joko Beck warns her students that embarking on a meditation practice can be like opening a personal Pandora's box. Over the years, we bury all kinds of unpleasant things in our psyches because we don't want to deal with them. But surrendering control to the moment means taking the leash off all this unpleasantness. Repressed feelings about your parents, regrets from a past relationship, personal failures ... whatever it is, expect it to rear its ugly head at some stage of meditation and trigger a strong reaction. I've often cried during meditation when painful thoughts or feelings arose. One of my nephews had a panic attack when he tried meditating. It's scary what can come up.

I remember being at a weeklong meditation retreat at the Springwater Center for Meditative Inquiry in Upstate New York. It was all silent, but there was an optional one-hour group dialogue each day. At one of these sessions, I reported that I was having a deep feeling of loneliness come up in my meditation, and it was very uncomfortable. One of the other people on the retreat was puzzled by this (as was I) and said, "Gee, I wonder why that's happening? We're all here together meditating. Why would loneliness come up?" But the teachers in the room had a different reaction. They saw it as an insight. "This is beautiful reporting that Chick is doing," they said. "What he's experiencing is true. It's real. He's not trying to comfort himself with some easy, fake answer like 'I'm missing my family.' No, he's getting to the root of his human experience."

What meditation provides that normal daily life does not is the time to sit with troublesome feelings such as loneliness that lurk just below our level of consciousness and haunt us. I noticed I was feeling lonely, which is the first step. Then I resisted the knee-jerk urge to dismiss or analyze it. Instead, I observed it without trying to control it. I let it do whatever it wanted to do, which in this instance was make me sad and uncomfortable. Joko Beck calls this "the burning out of thoughts by the fire of attention," which she says is the main purpose of meditation.

Loneliness didn't exit my life entirely after this episode, but, like any bully when confronted, it did lose some of its power over me. By becoming more objectively aware of this thing called loneliness, I was able to see that its power was never actual, it was *perceived.*

Part of what's happening in meditation is finally realizing that we are the source of our suffering—not him or her or this or that, but us. This is both the bad news and the good news. It is bad news that we are the source of our suffering because our minds so want to blame others or circumstances. But it's actually good news, wonderful news, that the root cause is within us. Why? Because if it is others or the world that is the cause, we are screwed! If I am destined to wait for everyone else and the entire world to do what I want them to do before I can be happy, I'm going to be waiting a long time! But if changing my perspective, my attitude, my thinking is the secret, then the potential is unlimited.

Whatever experience we've pushed away or repressed because it felt shameful, humiliating, or unbearable at the time is not here now. So why does it still cause us pain? Because we don't realize there is another possibility: we can simply let it go. But that's easier said than done. It takes practice to develop the ability to relax into difficult feelings, to allow them to be felt fully and move through us, and to release them without control or judgment. Once you learn to do so, tears of pain become tears of relief—and you'll be free.

> Pain, the price of freedom ... Once you look inside yourself and start to own this, you will see that you are back to the same two foundational choices. One choice is to leave the pain inside and continue to struggle with the outside. The other choice is to decide that you don't want to spend your entire life avoiding the inner pain; you'd rather get rid of it.
>
> What would your life be like if it wasn't run by that pain? You would be free.
>
> To live at this level of freedom, you must learn not to be afraid of inner pain and disturbance ... simply view inner pain as a temporary shift in your energy flow.
>
> This is the core of spiritual work.
>
> —from The Untethered Soul by Michael Singer

So, meditation is not all birdsong and laurel. It's risky. It takes courage. And it can occasionally get ugly. But if you can let go of your ego for once, forfeit control for once, and relax into whatever is happening, you just might find more there than you expected.

■ ■ ■

In the '80s, my friend Stew also introduced me to the Chogye International Zen Center of New York. It was founded by Seung Sahn, the first Korean Zen master to live and teach in the West. Seung Sahn came to the United States in 1972 (without money or a mastery of English) to deliver the message of Zen philosophy and practice to America. I started driving into Manhattan early on Saturdays to attend the morning practice at the center. I would don a robe, do 108 prostrations, sit for forty-five minutes of silent meditation, and have a short Zen interview with whoever the guiding teacher was that week. Zen interviews are fascinating learning experiences where you are given short koans (*kong-an* in Korean). These riddles (e.g., What is the sound of one hand clapping? or What was your original face before your parents were born?) cannot be answered by the Western mind's normal process of rational analysis. They are attempts to create an environment where the mind recognizes its own limitations and is forced to awaken to what was here prior to mind-created thought and form. This was my introduction to formal practice.

After attending a number of these Saturday sessions and a couple of daylong meditation retreats, I summoned the courage to try a weekend sleepover retreat. This upped the ante significantly. It involved ten total hours of meditation in thirty-minute intervals from 4:30 a.m. to 10:00 p.m. In between were times for silent walking meditation, eating, and resting.

I'll never forget my first night there. The Zen center was really just an apartment on the Lower East Side. (It's actually still there; my son Jamie recently attended the same Saturday morning practice I did with the same teacher, Richard Shrobe.) As I was sitting in the Friday evening silent meditation, I could hear Led Zeppelin blasting from a stereo in the adjacent apartment where a party was going on. I remember thinking, *How did I get from there to here?*

Later that night when everyone started getting ready for bed, I realized I was woefully unprepared. My colleagues had brought sleeping bags and nightclothes, but I hadn't brought anything. I don't know what I was thinking. I watched as they rolled out their bags on the floor next to each other, lay down, closed their eyes, and promptly fell asleep. Meanwhile, I was panicking: *Now what? How am I ever going to get through this night?* I strongly considered going home. What stopped me was the realization that the garage where I'd parked my car was closed for the night. Otherwise, I might have left.

It was a long night. When morning mercifully came, I had managed to doze off for a few hours at most. Dragging myself up, I watched again in fascination as my colleagues jumped out of bed and readied themselves for practice. I learned later that this is part of the Zen ethos—no lagging, no procrastinating, just doing without thought getting in the way. But when practice resumed, just sitting there with my legs and knees hurting, I noticed how much more relaxed and indeed happy my mind was for stretches of time. I found humor in the craziness of the situation, how far out of my comfort zone I was, and yet all was still fundamentally okay, no matter how much my thoughts tried to convince me otherwise. It was truly a mind-expanding experience, with no drugs involved other than sitting with my own misery!

I resisted becoming a member of the Zen center, however, as it required committing to five precepts, one of which was "I vow to abstain from intoxicants, taken to induce heedlessness." At that point in my life, I had no interest in or intention of doing that. Sobriety was for monks, not for me. I was okay doing a six-hour meditation retreat on Saturday, then going out that night and drinking and drugging to have fun. I saw no contradiction in doing that.

Unfortunately, I wasn't as balanced and in control as I thought I was, but we'll get to that later.

■   ■   ■

As I'm writing this book, I'm working on one of the biggest real estate deals of my career. Millions of dollars are at stake. It's a busy and exciting time. My son Cory works with me and watches how I react to stuff. When I'm bouncing all over the place, whining and complaining and getting upset, he'll go, "Where's the Zen guy, Dad?" And it makes me laugh. All I can say is, "Can you imagine what I'd be like if I didn't meditate?"

All kidding aside, I react how I react. I let it be as it is. And that is the practice. If I get a call that this big deal has fallen through, and if I understand why that happened, I may say, *This sucks!* and feel sad about it. If I feel the guy I've been negotiating with is being unfair, I may get angry. *He's being an asshole!* So, sometimes my reaction to things isn't very spiritual. I do continue to try and improve my negative reactions, to pause and respond rather than compulsively react. But it's important to first accept what happens. You hope that over time with meditation the reactions aren't as strong. But you're still going to react in some way. What I try to do, sometimes with more success than others, is to not take it out on other people. At the end of a rough day, sometimes the best I can do is not go home and kick the dog. I can't avoid feeling what I'm feeling, but I can avoid yelling at my wife or taking it out on my sons. And if I can do that, that's kind of a success. And tomorrow will be another day. As they say in AA, "*One day at a time.*" That's how I incorporate meditation in my daily life, and, I think, that's living a successful life. Joko Beck puts it this way:

> *Meditation isn't just sitting on a cushion for 30 or 40 minutes a day. Our whole life becomes practice, 24 hours a day.*

There's one more point I want to make before I close out this chapter, and it has to do with wonder. Meditation has helped me maintain some childlike qualities far into adulthood. (Childlike, not childish, which is very different.) These include playfulness, humor, humility, innocence, open-mindedness, and, perhaps most important, wonder.

The most beautiful thing we can experience is the mysterious. It is the source of all true art and science. He to whom the emotion is a stranger, who can no longer pause to wonder, and stand wrapped in awe, is as good as dead—his eyes are closed.

—ALBERT EINSTEIN

I couldn't agree more. If we never put down doing, where is our time to stop and wonder? When do we allow ourselves to be awed by the illogical, incomprehensible fact that we are here at all? To do so is to experience our true nature, our default state of being. And it is accessible to you right now through meditation.

To be yourself in a world that is constantly trying to make you something else is the greatest accomplishment.

—RALPH WALDO EMERSON

Sixth Awakening:

All I Can Do Is Live This Life to the Best of My Ability

MY MEDITATION PRACTICE was in high gear. My life was also in high gear. Ellen and I had our first child, Dan, in 1988, when I was thirty-two. Fifteen months later, our second boy, Cory, arrived. And then in 1995 we had Jamie when I was thirty-nine. No matter how prepared you think you are for parenthood, you're not. Having three sons in seven years was bewildering at times. But life was expansive and good on so many levels.

Ellen had been working full time as budget director at a local hospital, but she left that job after Dan was born and used her CPA license to join a more traditional accounting firm. This allowed her to work part time and have more flexibility. Meanwhile, my responsibilities at the family real estate company were growing. My older brother, Jack, had joined the firm first. But he was content doing the bookkeeping and letting our father run the business. I wanted to learn all I could about real estate, and Dad taught me everything, from dealing with tenants, banks, architects, lawyers, and contractors to understanding financial models. When my brother Bob joined later, he was also ambitious and motivated, so as the years went by and our father reduced his responsibilities, Bob and I ran the business together. We mostly did commercial real estate, but in 1986 we started a major ten-year project that involved building six hundred townhouses, one hundred and ten senior apartments, a retail center, and six office buildings, totaling over a quarter of a million square feet of space.

I was learning a lot, making good money and, for the most part, enjoying my work. It was a busy time, no doubt, but it was basically an eight-to-six job with weekends off. So, I was home in the evenings with my boys, and I had the weekends free to spend with friends and family. I coached each of my boys' Little League baseball and youth soccer teams in the spring and fall seasons. This was richly rewarding for me. My father was a confident, successful, self-made man, but he was not a workaholic and never expected his sons to be. I'm very thankful for that. His work/life ethic was work/life *balance*. He taught me that by example, by making sure no matter how busy he had been, he still showed up to watch my brothers and me in all our sporting events. To this day, I consider time to be the most valuable asset. Money is just a tool that allows you to buy back the ability to choose how you spend your time.

Like any family business, however, there were challenges, and these started building through my thirties as I acquired more expertise in real estate development. My father had a very strong personality and a huge amount of integrity, which is what drew people to him and made him successful. But he didn't do things by committee, and he was never wrong. When I first started working with him in my twenties, I was okay with that. I was headstrong and opinionated, too, but it was his company, so if we disagreed it seemed right to do what he wanted. But after ten years or so of that, it started to wear on me to the point where we'd get into arguments and I'd tell him, "Look, if you want me to handle this, then I'm going to handle it the way I want."

It never got so bad that I considered quitting (love was always there, and disagreements never lasted more than a day or two), but it was a source of tension and stress at a time when I already had plenty of that. Fortunately, I had my meditation practice to help me stay centered and keep things in perspective. I never lost sight of its importance and continued to prioritize it. I was also doing a lot of spiritual study during this time. Many of the quotes sprinkled throughout these chapters come from books I read during this period that shaped my spiritual philosophy. They continue to adorn the walls of my office, reminding me to keep a larger perspective on things.

I remember telling my parents that I was going to start attending the Zen center in New York that I mentioned in the last chapter. We were out for dinner, and I brought it up not knowing how they'd react. After all, my father was an army veteran and our family was Jewish, and here was their son talking about Zen Buddhism. But they were like, "Hmm, that's interesting. Why would you want to do that?" I explained that it was something I was drawn to, they listened politely, and then they said, "That's nice," or something to that effect, and we went on with our meal. So, in the family it was never an issue or a big deal.

However, there were two other things that happened when I was entering my fourth decade that "awakened" me in more conventional ways. The first was the death of my best friend, Dave. He was diagnosed with pancreatic cancer at age forty-one, and a year later he was gone.

My friend Steve introduced me to Dave shortly after I'd graduated from college. Steve and Dave were attending Penn Law School in

Philadelphia, and I'd drive there on weekends to hang out. Penn Law had a reputation for being impossibly hard, but Dave was cruising through, working with the bare minimum needed. He was a brilliant guy, probably the smartest person I ever met.

The video game *Space Invaders* was popular at the time, and Dave and I were both into it. Steve had the feeling we would get along great, and since we were the best players he knew, he concocted a plan for getting us together one night. His plan was to find a bar and have some fun playing *Space Invaders*. But one thing led to another, we partied late into the night, and the next thing I knew we were all back at Steve's apartment, it was 3:00 a.m., and we'd never gotten to play.

"Wait a minute," said Dave in his nonchalant kind of way. "I think there's a machine at this 7-Eleven in downtown Philly, and I'm pretty sure it's open twenty-four hours."

So, without a second thought, off we went, and, sure enough, it was open, and there was a *Space Invaders* inside. I couldn't believe it, but I soon learned that if Dave had a hunch, it was very likely true. I can't remember who beat whom, but we were there until dawn, and Dave and I became fast friends. Years later, Ellen and I bought a ski condo in Vermont with Dave and his wife, Sally. They had two boys, and we enjoyed many vacations together.

His death hit me hard. I struggled emotionally with it for a couple of years afterward, and I still miss him to this day.

The other thing that happened around this time was I developed severe neck and shoulder pain. I had been diagnosed with cervical stenosis in my twenties—a condition where the spinal canal is too small for the spinal cord. It had progressed to the point where it was pinching nerves and causing me a lot of pain—or at least that was the theory. After consulting with several physicians, some of whom recommended surgery, I landed in the office of John Sarno, MD, at the New York University School of Medicine. He was the head of rehabilitative surgery there and quite controversial.

Sarno had come to believe that most back surgeries were unnecessary and not helpful. He argued that most back pain resulted from repressed emotional trauma. The pain manifested physically because it wasn't socially acceptable at the time to express emotional pain. People were ashamed to admit feeling anxious or depressed. And mind-body medicine, as it's known today, was in its infancy. So, doctors took the conventional route and routinely prescribed surgeries for back pain, often with mixed results. Sarno had helped our friend Sally with difficult pain symptoms years earlier, and I was intrigued by his noninvasive approach. He ended up referring me to a psychotherapist, and, believe it or not, six months later my neck and shoulder pain was gone. No physical treatment, and I was able to resume all the activities and sports I loved.

This was my first experience with psychotherapy, and I found it to be an amazing tool. Spiritual practice is wonderful, and, as you've seen, it changed my life in many ways. I've already mentioned how letting uncomfortable memories and thoughts arise during meditation and observing their effects can ultimately free you from their grip. The more time you spend with them, the more you realize they are powerless and you can let them go. Therapy approaches these issues in a different way. Being guided by a mental health professional enables you to become conscious of what has been buried in your subconscious so you can finally see it and heal it. It's based on the idea that you can't begin to solve a problem until you acknowledge that there is a problem. I found therapy to be very helpful in this regard. It's not that I had an awful childhood where I was beaten or abused. To the contrary, my childhood was relatively happy. But we all have experiences in our past that continue to impact the way we process our current experience. Maybe you were bullied at some point, or perhaps your parents had some relationship issues that impacted you. Even small childhood humiliations can have a lasting impact if they are repressed and remain unreleased. It doesn't have to be brutal trauma to cause ongoing suffering.

The spiritual world is rife with people who have a lot of spiritual insight and who have supposedly been "enlightened" but who are emotionally repressed and could really have benefited from therapy. Look at the scandals surrounding such famous spiritual teachers as Bikram Choudhury, Yogi Bhajan, and Osho, to name just a few. The sexual and verbal abuse inflicted by these men is shocking. It doesn't mean they didn't possess spiritual wisdom. It just proves that believing it's a cure-all and that it makes you a whole human being without emotional issues is incorrect.

Jack Kornfield is a wonderful example of a great current spiritual teacher who recognized this. He studied Buddhism in the East, had huge enlightening experiences, and became a respected teacher. But upon returning to the United States and all the emotional baggage he'd left behind, he quickly realized he still needed help, went into therapy, and ended up getting a degree in clinical psychology. The title of his book *After the Ecstasy, the Laundry* kind of says it all. You can only live with your head in the clouds for so long; then you must deal with your shit. As Kornfield recounts in his book, Pir Vilayat Khan, head of the Sufi Order in the West, said it this way:

> *Of so many great teachers I've met in India and Asia, if you were to bring them to America, get them a house, two cars, a spouse, three kids, a job, insurance, and taxes ... they would all have a hard time.*

In my opinion, spirituality without therapy, or vice versa, will always be incomplete. To be truly balanced, peaceful, and whole, you need both. The integration of the two has been a wonderful contribution by Western society to the spiritual wisdom brought here from Eastern traditions such as Buddhism and the Hindu Advaita Vedanta.

Fortunately, I had these tools at my disposal during this period of my life. Many people recall their thirties and early forties as the "overwhelming years" because of all the stress that surrounds raising a family, building careers, and managing finances. But while there were plenty of *moments* when I felt overwhelmed, I wouldn't characterize myself as feeling that way overall. There was a lot more happiness than anxiety, even with everything that was going on.

Another thing that brought me joy and helped me keep my perspective during this time was travel, particularly adventure travel. Being outdoors in nature has been one of my abiding passions ever since those long-ago summers at Camp Scatico. As I've said, I never felt religious, nor did I experience the sacred while sitting in a synagogue or church. But hiking in the wilderness or rafting a river? That's where I've felt the presence of the divine, however that's defined. Being immersed in the grandeur and wildness of nature is soul nourishing for me.

My older brother, Jack, introduced me to whitewater rafting when I was in my early twenties. I joined him and his college buddies for a two-day trip down the Gauley River in West Virginia. We played hard and partied hard, and I loved every aspect of it.

I eventually rafted many rivers with this crew—the self-proclaimed Vishnu Vagabonds—including the Chattooga in Georgia, Youghiogheny in Pennsylvania, Upper Tuolumne in California, and Selway in Idaho. Bruce, who was the driving force behind these trips, often spoke reverently of the Biobío in Chile as the pinnacle of whitewater adventure. As it happens, I met a guy through work who was going to raft the Biobío, and I joined him. It was such a thrill that I returned to Chile with the Vagabonds a few years later to raft the Futaleufú River in northern Patagonia. I kept detailed journals during many of these trips, and they're filled with ruminations on my search for meaning and truth. In the last twenty years, biking trips with Ellen throughout North America and Europe have replaced these priceless rafting trips.

I have been telling Ellen and Mom and Dad that it is a safe trip. They are still nervous, and if the truth be told, I have some twinges myself. I do believe it is basically safe, but saying goodbye to Daniel, Cory, and Jamie makes me think twice about taking any risk whatsoever.

… These trips, though, are as inviting to me as anything I could possibly do. I look forward with great anticipation to the days and nights in the wilderness. To reconnect with nature, with sights and sounds, serenity, and wildness, calming and exciting at the same time, is vital to my soul.

—Excerpt from the beginning of my Rio Futaleufú trip journal

Bruce, Stan, Ron and I had a wonderful, interesting conversation at lunch. It began with Bruce asking me what topics I wrote about mainly in this journal. It flowed into all of our feelings about vacation, everyday life, responsibility, what is the nature of freedom, how one goes about attaining it and various other related issues. It was just the type of conversation that stimulates me. Unfortunately, the opportunity to have such a conversation comes much too rarely, but for which I'm grateful to this trip and these friends.

… The moon is staring at me just over the treetops on the far bank of the river in yet another cloudless, intensely blue sky. The morning light carries a richness to it which I forget in the rush of normal life. The river just below my feet appears to be breathing as it plies a gently swaying of the reeds.

… I talked to Cary a little bit about the search for meaning and self-understanding yesterday and the different possible paths towards it.

—Excerpts from my Selway River trip journal

I have no doubt that these adventures, combined with spiritual study, meditation, and therapy, contributed to keeping me sane and content during this time. I've always been self-aware, but there's good and bad that comes with that. On one hand, being a sensitive person helped me be more compassionate and empathetic. But on the other, ignorance is bliss, and I often wished that things I heard on the news or experienced in person wouldn't bother me so much.

There was no aha moment attached to this Awakening. Rather, it was a series of slowly learned insights. I gradually found my way to the understanding that *all I can do is live this life to the best of my ability*. I don't have to live this life perfectly. I don't have to be the ideal husband, father, or real estate developer. All I have to do is give it my best and try to be happy.

In his book *The Four Agreements*, Miguel Ruiz tells this story:

There was a man who wanted to transcend his suffering, so he went to a Buddhist temple to find a master to help him. He went to the Master and asked, "Master, if I meditate four hours a day, how long will it take me to transcend?"

The Master looked at him and said, "If you meditate four hours a day, perhaps you will transcend in ten years."

Thinking he could do better, the man then said, "Oh Master, what if I meditated eight hours a day, how long will it take me to transcend?"

The Master looked at him and said, "If you meditate eight hours a day, perhaps you will transcend in twenty years."

"But why will it take me longer if I meditate more?" the man asked.

The Master replied, "You are not here to sacrifice your joy or your life. You are here to live, to be happy and to love. If you can do your best in two hours of meditation, but you spend eight hours instead, you will only grow tired, miss the point, and you won't enjoy your life. Do your best, and perhaps you will learn that no matter how long you meditate, you can live, love, and be happy."

That simple realization took a lot of the pressure off me and, in retrospect, allowed me to cope and be relatively happy. And that willingness to let go of the striving and just appreciate the present with all the awareness I could muster at the time turned out to be enough—more than enough, actually.

Most of our experiences and feelings about our lives stem from our concepts about how life should be. Yet real life is not conceptual. Concepts are stories we make up in our heads. And they constantly bump up against and conflict with what is really happening in our lives and the world. How many young couples, for example, get into financial difficulty because their *concept* of success is a fancy new car or a home they can't afford? Or how many marriages fall apart because the people involved are more in love with the *concept* of living happily ever after and never realize they're not in the arms of a prince or princess and aren't willing to put in the time and effort to make the relationship work? Real life is not conceptual; the description is never the thing.

Always we hope someone else has the answer.
Some other place will be better, it will all turn out.
This is it.
No one else has the answer.
No other place will be better, and
it has already turned out.
—LAO-TZU

How did I find the time for spiritual practice, let alone therapy, during such a hectic time? The answer is simple. I never considered my life and my spirituality to be separate. I didn't have to put my life on hold while I immersed myself in the spiritual. Rather, the practice became bringing the spiritual into my daily life. That's what this book is all about. It's okay to go off to a yoga class or a Zen center or even to India for a monthlong retreat. But you can't stay there forever. (I guess you can, but would you really want to?) Sooner or later, you're going to have to come back to your misbehaving kids or your rush-hour commute (or the laundry, as Kornfield put it) and apply what you've learned.

Spirituality isn't about escaping from a situation; it's about learning to be in that situation fully.

So, along about now, you might be thinking, *This guy really has his shit together. He's quite the role model.*

Maybe you're even feeling a little envious.

Thank you for that sentiment, but I still had issues going on, like everyone else.

In the words of that old guru Macbeth, "Nothing is as it seems to be."

Recovery is ego deflation at depth.

—BILL WILSON, ALCOHOLICS
ANONYMOUS COFOUNDER

■ ■ ■

The difference between illness and wellness is
Illness starts with "I" and
Wellness starts with "We."

—AUTHOR UNKNOWN

■ ■ ■

One day at a time.

—ALCOHOLICS ANONYMOUS SAYING

■ ■ ■

God, grant me the serenity to accept
the things I cannot change,
The courage to change the things I can,
And the wisdom to know the difference.

—SERENITY PRAYER USED TO CLOSE MOST
ALCOHOLICS ANONYMOUS MEETINGS

Seventh Awakening:

I Have a Problem

ALCOHOL AND DRUGS had been a part of my life ever since college. Over the years, I used marijuana, LSD, mushrooms, cocaine, Ecstasy, quaaludes … you name it. Experiencing alternative states of consciousness was an extension of my exploratory nature and my ongoing quest to understand what life was all about.

At least that's one way to look at it (and one with some truth).

But the bigger reason I drank and partied was because it was fun and it made me happy. When I was drunk or high, my worries and fears left me. I was no longer a social wallflower. In my twenties, before I was married, I loved doing coke and quaaludes and staying out all night with my buddies. Quaaludes changed that wallflower into Casanova, at least for a night. During that time, I also discovered Ecstasy (or X). It's a well-named drug because that's exactly how it makes you feel. The joy and pleasure you experience is so great. I remember being on a beach in the Bahamas, just sitting there doing nothing, and thinking *This is the happiest I've ever felt in my life.* Believe me, for a neurotic Jew, that's quite a statement!

If you wonder why people use this stuff, it's because it works. Your levels of dopamine and other feel-good hormones go through the roof. While you're using, you feel incredible. There was no comparison between the high I got from meditating and the high I got from drugs. But like George Carlin said, "Cocaine makes you feel like a new man. Problem is, the first thing that new man wants is more cocaine."

My drug and alcohol use never became excessive, however. If I had pills, I'd take one, not five or ten. I avoided trouble with the law, never abused friends or family members, and remained functional during the week and didn't miss work. I was a happy imbiber. And after I got married and the kids came along, with Ellen's encouragement I gave up the more extreme substances—the coke, the X, my beloved quaaludes, and the weed, which had started making me anxious and paranoid anyway. But still, when I got home from work, I'd have a Jack Daniel's (or two) to relax.

But I never thought I had a problem. There's a lot of research that alcoholism and addictive behavior are inherited, but no one in my family ever struggled with any of that, as far as I know. And although I grew up in the 1960s and early '70s, I was completely straight through high school. I remember going to the Summer Jam at Watkins Glen in 1973 when I was seventeen. There were six hundred thousand people there listening to the Grateful Dead, the Allman Brothers, and the Band. Drugs were everywhere, but I didn't touch any of it. I may have been the only sober one there. But that changed in college, when I found myself in a frat house with sixty guys, and it continued after I graduated. Still, I always thought I knew how to manage it.

Until September 3, 2001.

That summer, Ecstasy became available to me again through a friend. I was forty-five and hadn't done X in fifteen years, but I still remembered how wonderful it made me feel, and that was a temptation I couldn't resist. So, without telling Ellen, I started occasionally taking it again, mostly before social engagements. But there was no hiding it. I'd start hugging and being overly friendly with everyone. Afterward, Ellen would ask if I'd done anything other than drink, but I would lie and say no.

This was a very busy time for me, and I loved the escape X provided. I had a lot going on at work, and my oldest son, Dan, was getting bar mitzvahed at the end of the month, which is a big deal in a Jewish family. We were planning a big party with lots of family and friends, and we wanted everything to be just right. I remember thinking, *Just let me get through all this, and I'll fess up to Ellen and stop.* That Labor Day weekend, Ellen and I were going to a friend's house for a barbeque, and I popped an X before we left. Ellen knew something was off, and when we got home, she asked me again if I'd taken anything. But I insisted I hadn't.

Now, I have never been a comfortable liar. Plus, I loved Ellen, and this was no way to conduct a relationship. I lay in bed all night, unable to sleep, fretting about what I was doing. Finally, I couldn't stand it anymore. As soon as she woke up, I confessed that I'd been taking Ecstasy all along.

Understandably, she was extremely upset and bitterly angry, and all hell broke loose.

Not just that night, but in the days afterward too.

On September 11 the World Trade Center buildings in New York were attacked. I was only thirty miles away in New Jersey and could see the smoke from my office. The whole thing seemed surreal. Looking back, it was like the external world was mirroring my internal chaos. Ellen and I were having the biggest fight of our marriage, and I felt myself crumbling along with those towers. And on top of all that, September 11 was Ellen's forty-sixth birthday.

It was an incredibly raw and fragile time. Although I loved my alcohol and drugs, I realized that lying was never okay and that I loved my wife and kids much more. And September 11 really drove that home. It didn't matter if on one level I thought I didn't have a problem; I clearly did. So, with Ellen's encouragement, I agreed to get professional help for my substance use.

I started by talking to a therapist who specialized in that. I was honest with her. I told her I couldn't wrap my mind around the idea that I was an addict. An addictive personality, yes. But an actual addict, no. I asked if I could address the issue through meditation. But she recommended a more direct approach: meeting with local drug counselors several nights a week.

The kids were thirteen, twelve, and six at the time, so we told them I was working late. Ellen and I smiled our way through Dan's bar mitzvah, and I don't think anyone noticed anything wrong—other than maybe me not having a drink in my hand.

The counselors turned out to be wonderful people, and despite my trepidation I got a lot out of working with them. For example, I mentioned how I was struggling with the "addict" label, and they explained that addiction is a spectrum, not just a word, and people are at many different levels. That helped a lot. And I asked them how you know when you have a problem, since there's no test you can take to determine it. And they said that one way to tell is when your morality is going in one direction and your behavior is heading in another. That hit home. I had always considered myself an honest and open person. Now I saw how my desire to use substances to feel good had become so strong it was making me lie to the person I loved most.

I believe the greatest positive event of the twentieth century occurred in Akron, Ohio, on June 10, 1935, when Bill W. and Dr. Bob convened the first AA meeting. It was not only the beginning of the self-help movement and the beginning of the integration of science and spirituality at a grass-roots level, but also the beginning of the community movement.
—M. SCOTT PECK, MD, IN *FURTHER ALONG THE ROAD LESS TRAVELED*

Eventually, after working with my counselors for about a month, they suggested I attend a couple of Alcoholics Anonymous (AA) meetings. I knew nothing about AA other than having heard the name, and I went to the initial meetings grudgingly. I told myself (and Ellen) I'd see how things went. I had no intention of getting a sponsor, making it a life thing, or buying in to any of their other crap. But what I began experiencing in those simple meetings blew my mind.

I was introduced to the Twelve Steps of AA. Reading them was another awakening for me. They were a path toward a spiritual awakening. Indeed, only the first step even mentions alcohol (or whatever addiction the program you're in deals with). And Step Twelve states, *"Having had a spiritual awakening as a result of these steps, we tried to carry this message to other alcoholics and practice these principles in all our affairs."*

I couldn't believe it. Here was a path to what I had been looking for, and it was in the last place I wanted to be. It occurred to me then (and many times since) that this brilliant solution to the problem of addiction is similar to the Buddha's Eightfold Path to Enlightenment and escaping suffering. I couldn't help thinking with wry amusement of the adage "be careful what you wish for because you just might get it, but not in the way you imagined."

I also appreciated how AA handled religion. The Twelve Steps are adapted from Christian principles, and a lot of the readings in the Big Book of AA have a strong Christian bias. I've never been a fan of organized religion, as you know, but AA made it about "finding a God of your own understanding." In other words, they softened it, allowing you the freedom to substitute any Higher Power you identify with, which is brilliant. (A few years into recovery, I heard the spiritual teacher Byron Katie define God as "Reality as it is." That really helped me find and embrace an interpretation of a Higher Power that worked for me.)

God is a metaphor for a mystery that absolutely transcends all human categories of thought.
—JOSEPH CAMPBELL IN *THE HERO'S JOURNEY*

And why do you prate of God? Whatever you say of God is untrue.
—MEISTER ECKHART, CHRISTIAN MYSTIC

And then there was the sharing that happened during meetings. Hearing people tell their stories so honestly really appealed to me. To hear other men, in particular, openly discuss their greatest fears, vulnerabilities, and humiliations moved me in a profound way. I entered recovery convinced that people don't really change. At our core, we are who we are. But then I met people with these incredible life stories. Some had been criminals and were now almost saints. Hearing their transformations made me realize that I had been completely wrong. People *can* change, and they can change dramatically.

I often tell people that how AA meetings are depicted in TV shows and movies and written about in articles never truly captures the uplifting energy and the atmosphere of love and support that pervades them. To understand AA, you must experience it firsthand. The world would be a kinder place if more people attended group meetings like these, where they would see the underlying humanity they share with those who look nothing like them and have completely different life situations and backgrounds.

From Yale to jail, from Park Avenue to park bench.
—AA'S DESCRIPTION OF THE DIVERSITY
OF PEOPLE WHO ENTER RECOVERY

So, I didn't quit after a few meetings like I thought I would. In fact, I ended up continuing with AA for eighteen and a half years, remaining sober that entire time. One of the million great AA aphorisms is, "How long do you have to keep going to meetings?" And the answer is, "You have to keep going until you want to keep going." And eventually, for all the reasons I just outlined, I started looking forward to them. They became a highlight of my day.

And there's another great AA saying, "Don't stop before the miracle," which for a lifelong seeker like me was just too big a promise to ignore. For those who stay, there's a complete psychic shift that happens. You see it in others, and you experience it in yourself. That's the "awakening" in AA. The program's basic teaching is that the use of substances is just a symptom of underlying emotional issues. That's why recovery is a *program*. You start by putting down the substances. And once you do that, you realize that everything else is still there. Another AA saying is "When you get rid of the alcohol in alcoholism, you're still left with the *ism*." *Ism* is an acronym for "I'm Still Me," meaning that all your crap is still there. That's when the real work begins. And if you stick with it, you change psychically, emotionally, and spiritually.

All this should sound familiar. Identifying the roots of our suffering and finally addressing them is the pathway to peace and happiness that I've been mapping throughout this book. Funny how so many roads lead to the same destination. AA turned out to be another approach to what I'd been pursuing. I've since met priests and rabbis who confessed that even with all their prior religious training, they never truly understood what it meant to lead a spiritual life until they joined AA and practiced its program of recovery.

Of course, after stating early on that I wouldn't get a sponsor, one day after I shared my story in a meeting, a man sitting in front of me turned around, extended his hand, and said, "Hi, I'm Bob." We started chatting. I told him about my struggle with all the God talk and said I was into Zen. He replied, "I love Zen!" and, before I knew it, I had a sponsor. We went to a weekly men's meeting together and then for coffee and talk. Those times were very special to me. He guided me through the Twelve Steps with great compassion and companionship.

One of the most beneficial parts of the program for me was Step Four, which involves making a moral inventory of your entire life. This includes all the resentments that you're still lugging around:

> *That person did xxx to me when I was eight years old!*
>
> *That teacher yelled at me!*
>
> *My parents made me xxx, and I'll never forgive them for it!*
>
> *My wife said I was xxx, and that hurt!*

Listing all these resentments—from major to minor—and voicing and examining each one in Step Five with my sponsor eventually gave me a whole new perspective on my life. By asking myself such questions as "What was my role in this?" or "What was really being threatened in me to cause such a strong reaction?" I came to realize what I was protecting and that I wasn't always the victim. It's a very action-oriented process, and anyone who takes it seriously can't help but see themselves in a new way.

Driven by a hundred forms of fear, self-delusion, self-seeking, and self-pity, we step on the toes of our fellows, and they retaliate.
—"HOW IT WORKS," BIG BOOK OF
ALCOHOLICS ANONYMOUS, PAGE 62

One of the most profound psychic shifts I experienced in AA was realizing how extensively fear had driven my behavior throughout life. I had awakened to that fact through my spiritual study and meditation, but this process helped me explore it in much greater depth. So much of my thinking and so many of my decisions and actions had been based on my fear of not being good enough or not winning another's approval. Why did I want people to like me? Why did I crave approval so much? Recovery helped reveal what was underneath all that for me.

It's one thing to talk about your resentments in a pop-culture way or to even sit with them in meditation, but to inventory yours and discuss them with others is another level entirely. To finally realize what's been happening in your life changes you. It's not that the fear or whatever you're dealing with magically disappears. Rather, you acquire the ability to recognize it when it returns and learn how to react. Fear doesn't have to rule you; you can just watch it, as we've already talked about, and say, "Wait a minute. What's underneath this?" And for me, to realize my level of fear and explore it from a different angle, and so deeply, truly affected me. And as you'll see in the next chapter, it opened the door to true enlightenment for me—an experience far beyond any high that alcohol or drugs could ever provide. Recovery enhanced the ability for these psychic shifts (some of which my spiritual practice had already started) to grow exponentially. It took me a step further toward realizing my true nature.

■   ■   ■

After I joined AA, Ellen and I also attended couples' therapy on and off for a while. Eventually, she attended some meetings of Al-Anon, a sister organization of AA for those impacted by another's substance abuse. We were both struggling emotionally during this time; there was a lot of anger that needed to come out. Another part of my psychic shift involved determining what in all this was mine and what wasn't. In other words, learning that it wasn't all about *me*. Al-Anon teaches the three *C*s about other people's behavior and feelings: you didn't *cause* it, you cannot *control* it, and you cannot *cure* it.

Even though it's easy to blame others (*They're the one with the problem!*), that's not reality. People in Al-Anon start to recognize this. They think they're going in to learn how to deal with a problem (e.g., their spouse or teenager), but they're quickly told to put that aside and look at themselves instead. *Let's sort your life out first, and then we'll decide what to do with this other person.*

Try what we have to give for thirty days. If you aren't 100% satisfied, we will gladly refund your misery.
—AL-ANON AND AA SAYINGS TO NEWCOMERS

Another big psychic shift for me was moving away from the shame-and-blame mindset that most of us walk around with: *It's either your fault, or it's my fault.* To open to the possibility that we can live without jumping to either of those extremes was a revelation for me. There is no blame. There is no shame. This is simply what's happening, and it's up to us to decide how to respond to it.

---

*People don't do things **to you**,*
People just do things.
—OVERHEARD IN AA

Part of this also involved learning not to immediately label a situation as a problem. Like *addict*, *problem* is just a word, and problems fall across a wide spectrum. In fact, some problems can be opportunities.

Indeed, many people go into AA thinking this is the worst thing that ever happened to them. It's a problem. But years later, after being exposed to this incredible spiritual process that is recovery, they describe it as the *greatest* thing that ever happened to them. It was an opportunity.

■　■　■

The spiritual journey is individual, highly personal. It can't be organized or regulated. It isn't true that everybody should follow one path. Listen to your own truth.

—BABA RAM DASS, SPIRITUAL TEACHER

In spring 2020, despite the affection and admiration I had for the AA program and the many benefits I'd derived from it, I decided to leave. This may surprise you after all the wonderful things I've said about recovery and the fact that many people remain in it for life. But I did not make this decision quickly or lightly. I had been pondering it for years. I discussed it with Ellen and each of my sons, as well as my closest friends and confidants in the program. Although Ellen and I had shielded the boys from what was happening at the time because of their ages, we had eventually discussed everything with each of them when the time was right, so they were well aware of my situation.

But being true to myself and my unique path was ultimately most important to me, and I felt comfortable leaving and resuming moderate alcohol use. I was fully aware that this ran counter to one of AA's core principles—that it's never possible for someone in recovery to successfully resume drinking. But I've never been comfortable with any all-or-nothing prescription. I never felt comfortable with the labels. When I spoke to one of my AA friends about what I was pondering, he said, "Chick, we both know that you aren't really one of us." Recovery drew me in for reasons beyond controlling my drug and alcohol use. AA was incredibly beneficial and positive for me in so many ways, and I recommend it heartily for those who are struggling, but it was time for me to leave.

Years before, I had started a weekly meditation group. I'll talk more about this in the next chapter, but many of my sober friends attended. I didn't want to lose them after leaving AA, so in the spirit of honesty that imbues recovery, I explained my decision and reasons with this note:

I'm writing this to all my meditation friends who are in Recovery.

I want to let you know that a couple of weeks back, after 18 ½ years of sobriety, I decided to step away from AA and bring casual drinking back into my life. I know this will bring shock, surprise, and disappointment to most or all of you, and I feel sad about that. This is not a decision I took lightly, or spur of the moment, or in a moment of weakness; it's something I've thought about for quite some time. I spoke with Ellen and each of my children, as well as a couple of trusted friends, before taking this leap into a somewhat new identity, walking away from totally sober Chick.

I love AA and the Recovery movement, and always will. I think it is one of the greatest forces for good on the planet. It taught me much about myself, the world, and how to relate to each in a mature, wise, and loving way. I also love the community of it and feel sad about making a choice which denies me access to it. But for myself, I was never fully comfortable with the one-size-fits-all, total-abstinence requirement of the program. I understand the importance of it for many, many people, but it has never felt like a natural fit for me, nor did the label "alcoholic" or the idea of having an "incurable disease." It goes without saying that I am only speaking for myself and trying to give people that I care about some understanding of where I am at.

It is my sincere hope that I can continue my relationship with each of you outside AA and that we will continue to meditate and dialogue together. I hope you can see through to my basic nature of goodness as I see yours, even if I have chosen a slightly different future path for myself. We must be true to ourselves above all, and that is what I look to have the courage to do.

I love and care about each and every one of you.

With love,

Chick

The response I received from the group was universally support-ive and heartwarming, and I still meditate weekly with all of them. My favorite reply came from one of my sober meditation friends who wrote back, "Wow, that's freedom! Absolutely you have my support."

So, on Memorial Day weekend 2020, I took my first drink in eighteen and a half years. It was a bourbon on the rocks, and it tasted nice, although I took that first sip with great trepidation. Ellen was there with me, although she doesn't drink anymore, along with my middle son, Cory. When he heard about my plans to leave AA, he said, "Dad, if you're going to do this, I want to be there with you when you have your first drink." In fact, Cory bought the bottle of Woodford Reserve for us to share.

And although it may not have been said aloud to the celebratory clink of glasses, I think we were all privately toasting to what we had survived as a family and to even better days ahead.

True freedom, however, is ultimately on the inside, as I was about to find out …

What you are looking for is What is looking.

—SAINT FRANCIS OF ASSISI

■ ■ ■

*The most vital task in your life is to
realize your essence identity.*

—ECKHART TOLLE

■ ■ ■

*The knowledge of our own being, its knowledge
of itself, is not only the most profound
knowledge possible but also the most precious.
It is the source of the peace and happiness
for which we long above all else, and the
foundation for the resolution of all conflicts.*

—FROM THE BOOK *BEING MYSELF*
BY RUPERT SPIRA

Eighth Awakening:

I See What I Truly Am

IT WAS A BEAUTIFUL LATE-SUMMER DAY in 2009, and I was frustrated.

Very frustrated.

I was at the Omega Institute for Holistic Studies, a spiritual center in the Hudson Valley north of New York City. It was the first day of a weeklong silent meditation retreat with the renowned spiritual teacher Adyashanti, along with about three hundred other seekers. I was fifty-three and had been sober for eight years. I had been meditating for more than twenty-five years and had attended about a dozen silent retreats at the Springwater Center for Meditative Inquiry near Rochester, New York. My inner life and perspective had been heightened in many ways, and my ability to handle life's ups and downs, stress and joy, was in a great place. But there was something missing, something that all the great spiritual masters spoke of but that I had yet to experience or fully understand. In Zen, yoga, and other traditions, it's called True Nature or the Essential Self. It is the ever-present, unchanging core—the "me" in all of us that stands above and before our emotional states and thoughts.

My journey to Omega started at Springwater about a year after I'd entered recovery. I'd stopped going to the Zen center in Manhattan on Saturday mornings years before because I was busy with the family and work. Springwater was founded by a woman named Toni Packer. One day when I was in Barnes & Noble, I happened upon her book *The Wonder of Presence*. I started reading about how she had once been a student of Zen Master Philip Kapleau, who had written one of the seminal Zen books in the West (*Three Pillars of Zen*). Kapleau had chosen Packer to succeed him as the head teacher at the Rochester Zen Center. But after reading Krishnamurti, she grew uncomfortable with the traditions surrounding Zen and especially the *teacher* and *authority* labels being applied to her. She eventually left the Zen Buddhist robes and rituals behind to follow her own path. This culminated in her opening what would become the Springwater Center.

Reading about how Packer had been impacted by Krishnamurti, as I'd been many years before, and her simple method of constantly directing attention back to current experience, without any preconceived notions, resonated deeply with me. It felt like she was carrying on the heart of Krishnamurti's teaching, and I really wanted to meet her. Since she was just several hours away, I signed up for a week of silent meditation at Springwater.

People looked at me like I had two heads when I told them my plans. *You're going to do what? You're going to spend an entire week not speaking?*

Honestly, I was nervous. I had never done anything that extensive or intensive. But I was really looking forward to meeting Toni because she seemed to have the same perspective I did. She questioned everything. The retreat began on a Friday evening. A couple dozen people were attending, and we all agreed to remain silent the entire time. The only exceptions would be the one-hour group dialogues each day and, if you desired, a twenty-minute private session with Toni.

I immediately signed up for that and got my chance to meet her one on one about midway through the retreat. When she walked into the room, she was dressed like any other woman in her sixties. Instead of having me bow to her as in traditional Zen interviews, she reached out and shook my hand. By dispensing with all the usual teacher-student formalities, she instantly put me at ease. I brought up Krishnamurti and the impact he'd had on me (and her), and she agreed that he was wonderful. But she cautioned me against putting him (or any teacher) on a pedestal.

Then I mentioned how I had been struggling for a long time with the idea of God. I told her I thought God was a concept, and she agreed. But then I admitted to being a little jealous of those who were able to believe so fervently because it seemed to bring them such tremendous peace. As an example, I singled out one woman at the retreat, a devout Christian who really believed in Jesus. And Toni said the simplest thing to me: "Yes, but, Chick, she is who she is, and you are who you are."

We chatted for a few more minutes, she hugged me, and I went back to my cushion. Within ten minutes of sitting back down, I was sobbing. Not just quietly to myself, but uncontrollably. I don't know what she had triggered in me, but I became very emotional. Then this feeling of peace and well-being came over me. It was unlike anything I had ever felt outside of a drug experience. All fear and anxiety left my body. I was just sitting there in bliss, and I carried that feeling around with me for the next day or two. It was incredible. Just her saying those eleven words made me feel, for the first time I could recall, that it was 100 percent okay to be completely who I was. As that insight sank in, it became humorous. Walking through the fields surrounding the center, I often found myself cracking up. *We're all going to die. What am I so worried about?* The need for approval that had dogged me my entire life had completely fallen away. It was hilarious to me how much I had struggled with that. It was all so suddenly silly.

Why did those eleven words affect me so deeply, as opposed to the eleven billion I'd read and heard previously? That is a question I can't answer, although I have certainly thought long and hard about it. Maybe the fact that I had been staring at the wood grain in the floorboards for six hours a day brought it on. Maybe the lack of sensory input made me more sensitive to anything spoken. Or maybe hearing it from someone whom I greatly admired and respected just hit home. Who knows? As I mentioned previously, the Buddhists say there are ten thousand reasons for everything that happens. For me, I guess, the time was just right.

My experience at Springwater was so moving that I've continued going there for weeklong silent retreats once or twice a year. I felt so comfortable there with Toni (she died in 2013) and then with the teachers who are carrying on the tradition. The experience also made me want to share my passion for meditation with others, and my colleagues in recovery were a fertile crowd. So, I started the meditation group I mentioned in the last chapter. It was very informal, just a half dozen of us initially, meeting every week in someone's apartment. We'd meditate silently for twenty minutes, read a passage aloud from a spiritual book that was popular at the time, and then discuss it. The interaction was great, and it contributed to what was probably the most introspective period of my life.

One woman who attended occasionally, Lisa, asked if I'd ever heard of or read any of the books by Adyashanti. I had not, but months later, when I was back at Springwater browsing through its little basement library, I came upon *Emptiness Dancing* and remembered Lisa's recommendation. Now you may assume that because of his name Adyashanti is some bearded, white-robed Indian sage. That couldn't be farther from the truth. His real name is Stephen Gray, and he grew up in California. I read *Emptiness Dancing* during the retreat and was greatly moved. He writes very plainly and clearly and is a gifted storyteller. As I read his book, it struck me that what he and other teachers like him were talking about was something I hadn't experienced. My feeling of bliss after meeting Toni might have been a taste of it, but it was definitely not the deep, life-changing realization of our True Nature that Adyashanti was writing about. The more I read, the more frustrated I became about missing this. And although I considered Springwater to be my spiritual home, I decided to find this guy and spend some time with him.

And that's how I came to be at the Omega Institute with three hundred other people on that beautiful late-summer day in 2009. Adya, as he's known informally, was on stage talking about the week of silent meditation ahead. He was a very unassuming character— slight, young, balding. It was both calming and exciting being in his presence, even though it was a huge auditorium. I was really hoping he would lead me to this essential insight that I felt I had been missing. So, I was determined, but after the very first meditation and dialogue session, my mind was all over the place. Even though I was in this beautiful setting with this great teacher, I was unhappy. I remember thinking, *I should have just gone on a golf trip like all my friends do. What's wrong with me that I feel compelled to do this stuff?*

I was so frustrated that during the next morning's session, after meditation and Adya's talk, I raised my hand during Q&A. He invited me to come up and ask my question. It was intimidating standing in front of such a large group, but I told him how frustrated I felt—that after a couple of decades of meditation practice, I still hadn't experienced what he and so many wise teachers were directing us toward.

He smiled and encouraged me to sit with my frustration, to just be with it, without judgment. He may have given me some additional similar advice but, to be honest, I can't remember it. His guidance was a bit disappointing because it didn't feel like anything new. As I walked back to my cushion, I didn't feel any different.

Well, I gave it my best shot, I thought as I sat back down. *I'll try what he says, but I've already been doing that.*

During his next talk, however, Adya told some stories. As I mentioned, one of his great strengths as a teacher is his storytelling ability. He related a conversation he had with his mother. She told him that even though she was in her fifties, there was a part of her that felt the same as when she was a young girl. Adya explained that even though she didn't realize it, she was talking about her True Nature. It never changes over time, remaining the same throughout our entire lives. And it never changes over space; we are still ourselves wherever we go.

We are always the same age inside.
—GERTRUDE STEIN

As I was sitting there in the auditorium, I thought, *Wait a second, I recognize precisely what Adya's mother is referring to. There is something in me that feels exactly the same as when I was younger, even though my body has clearly changed. The "me" that is in there experiencing my life feels the same, even though my hairline and other physical things and my beliefs have changed dramatically.*

Adya went on to say, "We refer to this thing called 'me' or 'I' hundreds of times a day. We think and talk about it constantly. 'I am going to eat lunch now. Man, that person was rude to me. I forgot to run the dishwasher last night …' Over and over, we think and talk about this 'thing' called 'me.'"

Then he added, "Don't you think we ought to know what we are referring to?"

He's right! I thought. *I think and refer to "me" constantly. How can I not know what that "me" is? It clearly isn't my physical body, otherwise I wouldn't think of it as "my" body. I'm the "my" part, not the "body" part. And it can't be my thoughts or emotions because they come and go. It must be something else, something more eternal. I am what experiences those things.*

And with that insight, a powerful shift started happening within me. I could feel the energy building. Yet my frustration was still there.

I continued pondering all this throughout the day and, as night fell, I found myself alone back in my tent cabin in the woods. I was pacing around with my thoughts and emotions, tired and still frustrated, waiting for fatigue to claim me. Then something happened, so swift and out of the blue that it's very hard to put into words. It was like a veil dropping. I saw *myself*—consciousness recognized its own existence. This "me" had no physical attributes, no personality, no emotion, no thought. It was merely a silent presence, pure awareness or consciousness. There was absolutely nothing personal about it. It was a completely impersonal aliveness.

This was not an out-of-body experience. I was still very much in my body; it did not disappear. But a realization flared up that this Conscious Presence was the feeling of "me" that I thought of or referred to, not the body or the personality.

*Everyone has the sense of "being myself." The
sense of "being myself" is our most ordinary,
intimate and familiar experience. It pervades
all experience, irrespective of its content. It
is the background of all experience.*
—FROM *BEING MYSELF* BY RUPERT SPIRA

All frustration and tenseness left me. Waves of joy rolled through
me, along with a feeling of being born anew and everything being
fresh. Watching my hand move or my foot take a step became the
most fascinating experience. Insights came flooding in, such as the
knowledge that *this is what everyone is! There is no other possibility. It
doesn't matter who or what anyone "thinks" they are; this is what they
really are! Indeed, this is what every sentient being is, not just us humans.
This is what life is!*

The meaning of all those impenetrable Buddhist sutras, including
the Heart Sutra I used to chant at the Zen center in Manhattan,
suddenly became crystal clear. They weren't just verses of mystical
fancy; they were descriptions of the True Reality. And my True
Nature was not being a husband, father, Jew, real estate developer, or
even spiritual seeker. Those were just descriptions of my human life
situation.

Human beings are storytellers. That's a gift we have. But it
becomes a curse when we believe that our stories are true. Some people
will defend their story with their life or kill you because you have a
different story. But life is not a story. Life is life. We are something
more miraculous and mysterious than a story. I have a real estate
career, a family, hobbies, and preferences, and this book contains
stories of my searching and awakenings. But that's not really me.

Those are descriptions of my personality and my life, but it's not who I truly am.

When I say I am free, I merely state a fact. If you are an adult, you are free from infancy. I am free from all description and identification. Whatever you may hear, see, or think of, I am not that. I am free from being a percept, or a concept.
—NISARGADATTA MAHARAJ, AUTHOR OF *I AM THAT*

Part of what was happening in my little tent cabin in the woods was that I was finally separating my Self from all my stories. I was seeing clearly for the first time what was behind them. What remained was what all the great sages and teachers had been writing and lecturing about for millennia, including Jesus and the Buddha. What that is has limitless labels—True Nature, Essential Self, No-Self, True Reality, Being, Consciousness, Awakeness, Life Force, God ... Whatever you decide to call it, it's not something that can be attained or created; it is the uncreated. It's something that has always been here, hidden in plain sight. No label can touch it, and nothing can contaminate it, stain it, improve it, or change it in any way. It is always pure, always awake, always aware.

*After his enlightenment, the Buddha passed a man
on the road who was struck by the extraordinary
radiance and peacefulness of his presence. The
man stopped and asked, "My friend, what are
you? Are you a celestial being or a God?"*

"No," said the Buddha.

"Well, then, are you some sort of magician or wizard?"

Again, the Buddha answered, "No."

"Are you a man?"

"No."

"Well, my friend, what are you then?"

"I am awake."

—FROM *SEEKING THE HEART OF WISDOM* BY
JOSEPH GOLDSTEIN AND JACK KORNFIELD

Part of my experience also involved no longer feeling separate from the rest of the world. A tremendous, reassuring sense of Oneness came over me. This is what every other person is and what every other dog, ant, and elephant is. This is the True Nature of all sentient beings. It was mind blowing. I had been looking in the mirror for fifty-three years, thinking I was seeing myself and believing I was separate from everything else, but that wasn't Chick! In fact, Chick doesn't truly exist. He is just an agreement among human minds! What exists is this Life Force or Consciousness manifesting through a physical body whose brain has manufactured all these explanations for itself, because it's incapable of grasping this True Nature. That is, until the veil drops. Then it's like you shed all your different personas as if they are costumes, and you finally realize your True Self.

The falling away of self is the most significant, bewildering, and liberating spiritual event in one's entire life, and perhaps the least understood.
—FROM *EXPERIENCING NO-SELF* BY ADYASHANTI

I realize this is not easy to understand. It's not easy for me to explain. But here's an analogy that might help. Realizing your True Nature is like realizing the principle of multiplication. When we are schoolchildren, we start learning addition and subtraction, and then we advance to multiplication. That's a tough idea to grasp at first. So, we start with ones and twos, and we memorize our multiplication tables. And eventually we reach the point where when our teacher asks "What's two times four?" we can quickly reply "Eight." Then we move on to higher numbers, and we keep memorizing those tables until one day something clicks. It happens at a different point for every child, but the veil drops, and we suddenly say, "Wait a minute. I get it!" And in that moment, we understand the *principle* of multiplication. We can stop memorizing those damn tables! Even if you ask me to multiply 256 × 27, I may need a piece of paper, but I'll be able to do it because *I understand the principle.* In fact, I don't just understand it, *I know it.*

The purpose of words is to convey ideas. When the ideas are grasped, the words are forgotten. Where can I find a man who has forgotten the words? He is the one I would like to talk to.
—ZHUANGZI, CHINESE PHILOSOPHER

This is the best way I can explain what happened to me at Omega. I finally just *knew*. I couldn't go to sleep that night. I was overwhelmed with energy and joy and laughter. Seeing everyone wandering around the grounds the next morning in silence, trying to be spiritual, working so hard to get somewhere ... it suddenly became hilarious. All this effort for something so simple. All this searching for something that was right here, right now! I stopped to sit on a bench for a while. It was a spectacular morning. I was so aware of everything, but it wasn't "me" that was aware. It was Awareness itself.

I felt this so deeply that I started sobbing again and had to go off into the woods. My soul had been looking for a place to rest for so long, looking here and there and everywhere. But there can be no real home or place to rest until you come to this. The search will never be over until you come to this. I was sobbing for that person I had been, that searcher who had been so blind to this.

I felt a tremendous sense of relief and peace, but at the same time I couldn't imagine what life could possibly be like after this.

There's no way it could ever be the same ...

*Everything will be okay in the end.
If it's not okay, it's not the end.*

—JOHN LENNON

Ninth Awakening:

I (Try to) Live What I Truly Am

I SPENT FIVE MORE DAYS AT OMEGA after the veil dropped. I was euphoric the entire time. As the Christians say, I was born again. But not in the traditional religious sense of that term. I was just seeing everything with fresh eyes. Omega is an old summer camp, and I remember watching this worker one morning approach a cabin with a paint can and brush. He started touching up the trim. Even this ordinary task seemed extraordinarily beautiful to me.

Everything is extraordinarily clear. I see that whole landscape before me. I see my hands, my feet, my toes, and I smell the rich river mud. I feel a sense of tremendous strangeness and wonder at being alive. Wonder of wonders.

—BUDDHA

The retreat ended with a big luncheon. After being silent for an entire week, everyone in the dining hall was chatting loudly about their experience and where they were heading next. I was sitting there, still silent, listening to the conversations, and thinking, *They don't see it. They still don't know.*

It wasn't that I felt superior. It's not possible to be smug when you realize you're essentially the same as everyone else. It was just an observation, and one that I found amusing. We had finished a week with one of the great spiritual teachers of our time, pledging to open ourselves to transformation, yet the major topic of conversation was "Are you going to see him next month in California?" Instead of letting go of their identities, these people had taken on a new one— that of spiritual seeker or "follower of Adyashanti." I recognized it because I had adopted a similar story for my life. I had thought I was going somewhere too.

Who cares about another retreat? No offense, but how many times do you have to hear or read the same thing? Why would you need to go anywhere when it is all right here?

I called Ellen on the drive home. We hadn't spoken in a week, and she asked, "How was it?"

"I don't know how to tell you," I said, laughing, "except that I found what I was looking for."

"Bliss?"

"No, it's not just bliss. It's this knowledge that I'd been missing, and then suddenly it was there, and I had these insights into certain truths. And I was free of identification with my personality. Everything faded …"

I was rambling and laughing, and Ellen didn't know what to make of it. Then, for no apparent reason, I blurted out, "And I'm sorry for all the times I was an asshole, and I'm sorry for all the times I might be an asshole in the future."

I think our conversation ended on that note, probably because Ellen thought she was talking to a man possessed, which I was, to a certain extent. As my life stories and identities had fallen away, True Nature had taken "me" over. Not literally, of course, but what was always present behind the thought-created "me" had been revealed. When I got home, I was in a different state, and it lasted for months. I'd look at everybody, and instead of just seeing their faces, I saw the emptiness that was looking out from behind their eyes. We are not separate things; our actual experience is unbounded.

Douglas Harding was an author and spiritual seeker who became obsessed with finding his True Nature. One day he came upon a self-portrait by an Austrian philosopher, Ernst Mach, that fascinated him. Instead of using a mirror to draw himself, as most artists would, Mach used his own point of view. As a result, his self-portrait didn't have a head.

That's when the veil dropped for Harding. When we're not looking in the mirror, we are also "headless." Try experiencing this right now. Take off your glasses or your hat, if you're wearing any, and notice that although you can see the rest of your body, you can't see your head. Our experience in every moment is as a Field of Awareness. This is the "Headless Way," as Harding came to describe it in his books. It's not mystical; it's very practical. And this is what I was experiencing. I saw that what was looking out from me, and from everybody, was True Nature, Pure Consciousness, Life Force, or whatever you want to call it. You're not Joe or Caroline, and I'm not Chick. We are all This.

I wanted to spend as much time as possible with this Pure Consciousness. I'd go about my usual daily tasks, but after they were finished, I had no desire to turn on the TV or read a book or scroll the internet like I used to do. All I wanted was to find a quiet room in the house, sit down on my cushion, and be with This. *Why would anyone want to distract themselves from **This**?* It was so magnificently blissful; I'd sit for hours.

This is the time, I suppose, when some people who've had a similar enlightening experience decide to drop out of society and move to India. I may have thought about doing that when I was younger, but I never considered it when I got back from Omega. I already had a life, a career, kids in college, and a wife I dearly loved who I would never walk away from. Saint Francis de Sales once said "Bloom where you are planted." I resumed my previous life with no regrets, but I brought a fresh perspective to it. I was still going to AA meetings and running the little meditation group, and I shared what I'd learned about spiritual awakening. I created a blog (chicksspiritual-blog.blogspot.com), writing dozens of essays on the insights flooding into me. I genuinely wanted to help everyone "see" in the way that I was seeing. I nearly drove my closest meditation friends crazy with my passionate exclamations: *"No, it's not that we're asleep and need to wake up; we are already awake! We are always awake! You just need to realize it!"*

A woman in the meditation group named Kathy, who was about thirty years sober at the time, came up to me one day and said, "Chick, something has happened to you. Something has changed. And I'm not the only one noticing."

It's not that I suddenly had an aura or light around me. I just understood the "principle of multiplication" and could now talk about it from the teacher's point of view. Nothing had changed externally. To everyone, I was still a balding, middle-aged real estate developer from New Jersey. But internally, I felt driven to share my experience with others in the heartful hope that they would awaken too.

Before Enlightenment, one reads holy books to see if you're getting it right. After Enlightenment, one reads holy books to see if they are getting it right.
—ZEN MASTER SEUNG SAHN

During this time, to better understand and integrate what was happening to me, I reached out to some prominent teachers of nonduality. This is an ancient Eastern philosophy that means "not two." It refers to the underlying Oneness of everything, which is what I was experiencing. Our minds separate objects by labeling them "this" or "that." Thus, we create opposites: large/small, smart/stupid, fat/thin, hot/cold, etc. Then we go a step further and choose which label in these sets of opposites we either approve or disapprove of. Nondualism points us back to the inseparable, interconnected nature of all reality.

The day you teach the child the name of the bird, the child will never see that bird again.
—KRISHNAMURTI

Among the teachers I spoke with were Scott Kiloby, author of *Love's Quiet Revolution* and founder of the Kiloby Center for Recovery. We met in Manhattan and became friends, and I ended up inviting him to New Jersey to give a talk and stay at my house. I also spoke with author and meditation teacher Loch Kelly in New York City. And after watching videos of the nondual teacher Rupert Spira on the internet, I called him up and arranged a video session of my own to help process my understanding. Then I went upstream to Rupert's teacher, Francis Lucille. His teacher was Jean Klein, who helped bring

Vedantic (nondual) philosophy to Europe and the United States in the 1970s and '80s. I spent a couple of weeks with Lucille at retreats in southern California and Florida.

All these teachers widened my understanding of what was happening and influenced my thinking.

■   ■   ■

Let's remove the spiritual aspect from our discussion for a moment because it can sometimes get in the way of understanding. Plus, as I experienced, the spiritual buzz fades. But after the euphoria, something very practical remains. I was left with a knowledge. It's still strongly present in me, and I continue to see the world from that perspective to this day.

What I'm trying to say is that once you understand the principle of enlightenment—that we are not our stories, our thoughts, or our beliefs—it can be applied in very pragmatic ways. For example, when we look at the world, we realize that we're killing each other over *beliefs*. The Russians believe their system of governance is better than ours (and vice versa), and we are both willing to go to war over it, as has happened in Ukraine. And it's been that way since the birth of man.

This single bit of knowledge—understanding that enlightenment is a path to personal happiness *and* a moral imperative for the well-being of humanity—takes it beyond the spiritual and drops it firmly into the challenges we're facing today. It reminds me of the first book I read by Krishnamurti all those years ago, *The Only Revolution*, in which he points out that replacing one government, economic system, or leader with another may improve things in the short term, but there is no system that will fundamentally alter the course of humanity—only a revolution in consciousness.

When I was attending the Zen center in Manhattan, the founder (Seung Sahn) wrote a letter to the pope that someone posted on the bulletin board. This was back in the 1980s when there were lots of protests against nuclear energy. His letter was so profound I never forgot it. He wrote, *"The greatest danger to humanity is not nuclear power, it's the nuclear power of our opinions."*

He was referring to our duality of beliefs—Russia versus the United States, Democrats versus Republicans, Catholics versus Protestants, Jews versus Arabs, religion versus science, you versus whomever you're warring with … No matter how passionate we are about something, we should never make it us against them. There is no enemy. There are just people who see things differently. When you make it us against them, no matter how much good you think you're doing, you're participating in the problem as opposed to the solution. This belief in our separateness is what's dividing us—and dooming us.

I think it's a great spiritual practice to turn on the TV and listen to the guy you hate most, the one who triggers you most. When you can see God there, you're getting it. If you have to turn off the TV every time you see the person, and he sends you into skyrocketing anger, you have a lot of waking up to do.
—ADYASHANTI, FROM *EMPTINESS DANCING*

I'm not advocating passivity in the face of perceived wrongdoing or not taking action to help achieve what you believe benefits society, humanity, or the planet. What I'm saying is that if you act from an inner state of seeing those who disagree with you as the "enemy" or "evil" or "against God's Will," then you are exacerbating the problem. This always applies, even in those circumstances where we need to fight against perpetrators of genocide, or in other situations where emotional delusions supposedly justify killing or subjugation.

I have always been moved by the story of Dietrich Bonhoeffer. He was a Lutheran pastor in Germany during the rise of the Nazi party. Even though one of his core values was pacifism, he refused to stand by while atrocities were being committed around him. He joined some military officers in a plot to assassinate Hitler. They were caught and eventually hanged by the Nazis shortly before the end of the war.

I recount this to again emphasize that these ideas are not a call to be passive; rather, I am pointing out the importance of the inner state from which right action springs. While Bonhoeffer's religious beliefs did see the Nazi actions as evil, he acted not out of hatred but rather out of a sense of moral and ethical duty. And he understood that what the moment before him demanded was more imperative than holding on to an identity as a nonviolent man.

I read an article this morning of yet another horrible incident in which a young, unarmed black man was beaten to death by five black police officers. Among the usual passionate condemnations and expressions of outrage, the article quoted one retired police sergeant who, in lamenting the inexperience of the officers involved, said this: "Human beings, man, that's what happened. They let their emotions get the best of them, and there was no veteran officer there to stop them. Usually when vets are there, things go differently because we have that experience to say, 'I understand you're mad, but you got to stop, you can't do this, it isn't right.'" And I thought, *That's an enlightened point of view. He understands that the perpetrators aren't monsters or demons, they are human beings like you and me, whose life experience and training didn't allow them the control over their emotions to see the horror of what they were doing.*

If you want to see the brave, look at those who can forgive. If you want to see the heroic, look at those who can love in return for hatred.
—FROM THE HINDU SCRIPTURE THE BHAGAVAD GITA

We are made of the same stuff. Although opinions differ dramatically, we are all looking out from the same inner Presence. This is the true Holy Spirit. So what is the point of warring against ourselves?

Deep down, I think we all sense this. Wherever you may travel in the world, for the most part people are people everywhere you go. Strip away their different belief systems and egos, and we all just want to love and be loved, to be happy and spread happiness, to be sheltered and give shelter to others. A big part of my Awakening was coming to see—and *feel*—this shared humanity. Once I became aware of this connection, things shifted on an everyday level. I stopped being so invested in being right. I stopped feeling embarrassed when I was wrong. I started listening to other opinions.

And you know what? A miraculous thing happened. For my entire life, I had been trying to change the world to fit Chick's point of view. And I hadn't gotten anywhere. But when I flipped things around and changed my point of view to fit the world, suddenly the world began to change.

This is the way I'm trying to live what I truly am.

A simple idea enacted through simple actions.

*If we could change ourselves, the tendencies
in the world would also change. As a man
changes his own nature, so does the attitude
of the world change toward him.*
—MAHATMA GANDHI

*We can do no great things, only
small things with great love.*
—MOTHER TERESA

■   ■   ■

Life's journey had brought me around the Zen Circle of Enlightenment. There are four points on the Circle. At the bottom or beginning (0 degrees) is normal state of mind. Things are what they appear to be. Mountains are mountains. Rivers are rivers.

At 90 degrees, perception starts to shift. The observation arrives that things are ultimately empty of meaning and existence. Mountains are only mountains, and rivers are only rivers, because we label them as such.

At 180 degrees, this emptiness is experienced, and we awaken to Emptiness being the Consciousness that is all things. Mountains are rivers. Rivers are mountains. *We* are mountains and rivers.

At 270 degrees, the experience of the Emptiness that is Consciousness deepens into an almost magical realm, where the miraculous becomes reality. Mountains move. Rivers flow upward. Guys with brushes paint trim.

At 360 degrees, you're back to where you started. You've returned to life as you once knew it. Mountains are back to being mountains. Rivers are once again rivers. But because of what you've been through, nothing is the same *because now you understand.*

This is how I felt returning to everyday life after Omega. I had been around the Circle. And after the buzz faded, I was left with this deep Knowing. And it has never left me. It remains, and it pervades.

Being right back where you started is certainly ironic, but that's the point (and what I find humorous). All the effort, all the seeking, all the reading, all the sitting, all the teachers, all the fancy concepts, even the Awakening itself, just lands us right back where we began.

Here I am, just being myself.

… BUT …

Here I am, being my Self.

I remember Krishnamurti saying that if it's an extraordinary experience you're after, then just take a drug. It's quicker. But if it's enlightenment you're after, then don't be surprised when you're ultimately left with ordinary experience. That's where the real work begins. Once you go around the Circle, your mission (if you choose to accept it) is to apply the change in you to your everyday interactions with the world.

I've found it frustrating at times. I'm still just a human being, after all. I am most certainly not an Enlightened or a Fully Realized Person, whatever the hell that means. Just ask my wife or kids, and they'll happily confirm that for you. At my sixty-fifth birthday party, my sons got up together and toasted (or should I say roasted?) me, saying things like, "One of Dad's favorite books is *The Four Agreements,* and he really embodies it. He never gets upset—except when he gets some negative news at work. And he never takes things personally—except when we do something he doesn't like ... Hmm, maybe we should talk about something else?"

It's so annoying when people know you so well! But I loved every minute of it, because behind their teasing their loving hearts were on full display. And what more can a parent want than to raise a new generation with loving hearts?

While spiritual and emotional states come and go, I know I can always return to resting in simple Awareness. That's my anchor. Once you've experienced it and know it, it's always there. It's the only fundamental truth. Everything else is relative. Even all the fancy philosophical pronouncements from prominent spiritual teachers are just relative concepts. In fact, they often contradict each other.

Because I *know* This, I no longer consider myself to be a spiritual seeker. But I haven't stopped doing retreats or going to Springwater. Maybe old habits are just tough to break, but I have friends there, and the experience is still meaningful to me. Two of the teachers at Springwater, Sandra and Wayne, once asked me, "Why do you keep coming back? For that matter, why do *we* keep coming back?"

The best answer I could give them, and another reason I've written this book, is because it lights me up. Talking about it, interacting with others who are interested in understanding this stuff ... there's great joy for me in that. Even though I don't identify as a spiritual seeker anymore, I certainly don't know everything, and I want to continue learning and growing. The veil dropping is not the end. It is a fresh start, a new beginning, an opportunity to start a little revolution. I've been lucky enough to stumble upon something that most people have not realized, and I want to share it with them.

Unfortunately, although I wish it were different, I can't tell you how to realize it. This isn't the part of the book where I deliver the action steps. Spiritual awakening or enlightenment is an accident. It takes passion and patience. For the very rare people I consider enlightened (Byron Katie and Eckhart Tolle, to name two), there was no logical reason for why or when enlightenment occurred. Katie, for example, battled years of depression, rage, and low self-esteem before literally waking up one morning on the floor with insight. She describes the experience as having "It" wake up and look through her eyes (the "It" being her True Nature or Consciousness).

But this isn't to say we can't make ourselves more accident prone. Meditation, spiritual study, and programs like AA can prep us, as they did me. But it'll happen when it happens.

Living a "normal" life after Awakening is one of the most profound tasks for a human being, integrating the direct religious experience into one's everyday life and interactions, nothing special yet no longer the same. It's a lifetime's journey, but one that's filled with gratitude and compassion for all.

I'll end with a selection of lines from one of my favorite spiritual poems.

"Happiness cannot be found through great effort and willpower, but is already present, in open relaxation and letting go.

…Although peace and happiness do not exist as an actual thing or place, it is always available and accompanies you every instant.

…Wanting to grasp the ungraspable, you exhaust yourself in vain. As soon as you open and relax this tight fist of grasping, infinite space is there-open, inviting and comfortable.

…Nothing to do or undo, nothing to force, nothing to want, and nothing missing- O! Marvelous! Everything happens by itself."

—From *Free and Easy: A Spontaneous Vajra Song* by Gendun Rinpoche

The shift from our habitual stories of the self to new ones is part of the process of liberation, but it does not stop there; we must even go beyond such liberation. It's not that the old stories are delusion and the new ones are enlightenment; rather it's that clinging to the old stories is deluding and not clinging to them is enlightening. By forgetting our old cherished stories, then each and every story that arrives at our doorstep enlightens us. But if we attach to these enlightening stories, delusion and suffering are re-established.

—TENSHIN REB ANDERSON, ZEN TEACHER

Epilogue

MORE THAN A DOZEN YEARS have passed between my awakening at Omega and the writing of this book. Life goes on. And so do its joys—and challenges.

Starting around 2006 and compounded by the 2008 recession, my family real estate business hit some difficult times. Along with our commercial properties, we had built several very high-end homes to sell in wealthy New Jersey areas, and when the housing market crashed, we lost a lot of money on those ventures. We were in debt for millions of dollars and didn't have a clear way of paying our lenders back.

I've talked about how we create identities for ourselves and how awakening enables us to shed these identities and connect with our True Nature. But this, too, can become a new identity story if we're not careful. And I still had a good part of my identity tied up being a managing partner of the Atkins Companies.

Fortunately, because of our reputation, we had a good relationship with the banks. They knew we hadn't done anything wrong; it was just bad timing. So, they were willing to work with us. And fortunately, we still had commercial properties generating revenue, and that helped keep us afloat.

But it was rough for nearly a dozen years. My lifestyle changed considerably. We scaled back our purchases and vacations. The entire family was affected, including my sons and brothers. But everyone pulled together and did their part. One by one, we made our payments. And eventually we became whole again.

Just as we were beginning to pull out of debt in early 2019, my eldest brother, Jack, died of cancer. I wish he had lived to see the company become successful again, but it wasn't to be. He was seventy years old, and his death saddened me greatly.

Then, toward the end of 2022, while I was writing this book, I had my own health scare. I'd been experiencing occasional stomach pain for about a year but hadn't thought much of it. But the Sunday after Thanksgiving I ended up in the emergency room with severe pain. The following morning, I had emergency abdominal surgery for a twisted bowel and a ten-centimeter mass in my intestine. Although I recovered from the operation quickly, and the doctor assured Ellen and me that he didn't "think" the tumor was cancerous, we spent an anxious two weeks awaiting the biopsy result. Fortunately, it came back benign.

So, shit happens even after enlightenment. You're not immune to life. As the Buddha preached, "All human beings without exception face sickness, old age and death." It's easy to be happy when things are going your way. But when you're looking at potential bankruptcy or a loved one dies or a tumor the size of a baseball just got removed from your gut, that's where the rubber really hits the road.

My spirituality sustained me through these difficult times, as did AA meetings, my Friday-morning meditation group, and the occasional weeklong silent retreat. It really helped to get away to Springwater. With my personality, it takes two or three days of quiet for my mind chatter to settle down. Those silent retreats enable me to stay balanced.

I don't want to give the wrong impression, though. It's not that the last dozen years were all hardship. To the contrary, there was a lot of joy and happiness in there. Most of the time I felt extremely blessed to have a loving wife, wonderful children who had turned into amazing young men, and a network of friends and family members I could rely on. No doubt my years of spiritual practice helped remind me of this and keep things in perspective.

I learned that just "suiting up and showing up," as I'd heard in AA meetings, is a profound approach to dealing with life's inevitable situations. Labeling them "situations," as opposed to "problems," in itself changes how we respond. I repeated the Serenity Prayer many times to myself (and to Life) during these years, even though I had no idea who I was talking to. One wise counselor had told me with a smile, "That's okay, just mark it General Delivery!"

What else have I learned? It's the little things that make the biggest difference—like having a heart-to-heart with your partner, calling a friend, or just relaxing into the present moment and taking deep breaths. By relaxing into the moment, I was relaxing into pure awareness, which is what we all are. And there's a deep reassurance there that we are not our troubles and we are greater than our life situations, and our minds learn not to "catastrophize" them. This doesn't mean you don't feel the sadness and stress; it's just that you understand there's much more beyond it. You learn to understand what Saint Francis meant when he said "Wear the world like a loose garment."

So, all the searching and reading and meditating, to where does it bring us?

It brings us back to being comfortable with who we are, no matter the situation.

Ha! How about that? All the yearning and looking everywhere to find truth, peace, and happiness, and the endgame is acceptance of ourselves and the world as it is.

Popeye was right after all: "I yam what I yam and that's all I yam."

And that is good enough!

CHICK ATKINS

AN UNLIKELY GURU

FEBRUARY 14, 2023

Thank you.

Recommended Reading

Although I've mentioned and quoted from many books in the preceding chapters, here are the ones my meditation group has enjoyed and benefited from over the years:

- *The Zen of Recovery* by Mel Ash
- *Awareness* by Anthony de Mello
- *The Four Agreements* by Don Miguel Ruiz
- *Emptiness Dancing* by Adyashanti
- *The Power of Now* by Eckhart Tolle
- *The Untethered Soul* by Michael Singer
- *A Thousand Names for Joy* by Byron Katie
- *Radical Acceptance* by Tara Brach

Plus, books that have helped me along the Way:

- *The Man Who Tapped the Secrets of the Universe* by Glenn Clark
- *The Only Revolution* by J. Krishnamurti

- *Everyday Zen: Love and Work* by Charlotte Joko Beck

- *The Wonder of Presence* by Toni Packer

- *After the Ecstasy, The Laundry* by Jack Kornfield

- *Wherever You Go, There You Are* by Jon Kabat-Zinn

- *Waking Up* by Sam Harris

- *Being Myself* by Rupert Spira